Germania

A Captivating Guide to the History of a Region in Europe Where Germanic Tribes Dominated and How It Transformed into Germany

Free Bonus from Captivating History
(Available for a Limited time)

Hi History Lovers!

Now you have a chance to join our exclusive history list so you can get your first history ebook for free as well as discounts and a potential to get more history books for free! Simply visit the link below to join.

Captivatinghistory.com/ebook

Also, make sure to follow us on Facebook, Twitter and Youtube by searching for Captivating History.

Contents

Introduction

Germany is a relatively young nation-state. United in 1871, it's even younger than the United States. However, the territories inhabited by the Germanic people have a rich history that reaches far back in prehistory and antiquity. Located in the heart of Europe, Germany witnessed centuries of conflicts, immigration, and negotiations. Consequently, its shape, size, and ethnicity changed throughout history. The territories which constitute Germany today were often war zones, and at times they would join forces against a common enemy or break apart due to internal conflicts. Because of these conflicts, Germany's boundaries, as well as what it means to be German, fluctuated throughout history and, in some way, are still evolving. The region's long and troubled history influences its present, its politics, and its nationality.

Today's Germany is situated on a historic migratory path. The first evidence of humans traces back fifty million years. First, distant relatives of modern humans migrated into these parts of Europe. Soon, they were followed by the Neanderthals, who were named by the valley in Germany where they were first discovered. Within the last few years, some of the biggest and most important prehistoric findings happened in today's Germany. Modern scholars believe that southern Germany could be the birthplace of music (and art in general) over 35,000 years ago. But the migration didn't stop with the arrival of the Cro-Magnon, the early humans. It continued through the centuries and even millennia. The Bronze Age saw the arrival of the Celtic people, whose civilization in central Europe survived centuries. At approximately the same time, the first Greek and Roman writers started describing the peoples occupying the territories of central Europe and, with these writers, the historical records of the area begin.

From around 300 to 500 BCE, the first Germanic-speaking groups of people started arriving in this region. They came from the east, and they encountered the Celts already living in the territory of modern-day Germany. Even though there were some similarities between the two ethnicities, the Germanic peoples slowly pushed the Celts back and started occupying the territories along the Rhine and Danube, previously controlled by the Roman Empire. According to the Romans, the Germanic tribes were warmongering people, determined to inflict fear and destruction upon the civilized world. The various peoples of Germania, the shadowy land beyond the borders of the civilized Roman Empire, were simply placed under the common name barbarians.

Once the conflict with the Romans was over, the Germanic tribes took the opportunity to rise into a new European civilization. The Franks were the first to attempt unification, and they managed to bring some of the Germanic tribes under their direct or indirect authority. At the same time, the Christianization of the pagan Germans began. Believing they were the heirs of the Roman Empire, the Frankish rulers built the foundation for the Holy Roman Empire. Starting in the 800s, the political structure of this empire that gathered various Germanic tribes into a loose confederation would shape the politics of Europe until modern times. With the dissolution of the Carolingian Empire, a new ruler, Louis the German, rose to power in the east, founding the first Germanic state in central Europe. His successors would become

Holy Roman Emperors and lead the German-speaking people into a modern future.

But the unity of the Holy Roman Empire was shattered during the 16th century when Martin Luther protested the Catholic Church. This conflict divided Germany and, with it, the whole of Europe into two rival factions: the Protestants and the Catholics. The Thirty Years' War of the 17th century was the culmination point of this conflict. The German territories suffered devastation and depopulation, and at the end of the war, the authority of the Holy Roman Empire diminished. Unable to control the territorial autonomy of each Germanic region, the emperor allowed his empire to become an arena in which various princes fought for dominion. Because of these conflicts, Prussia emerged as a military state in the north and Austria as the powerful Habsburg heartland in the south. At the same time, the waking of the German nation occurred. This rise of German nationalism would seal the fate of Europe in the future.

The modern history of Germany starts with the Napoleonic Wars and the resulting revolutionary army, which brought the Holy Roman Empire to its end. In its place, the ambitious German nation-state was founded by the Prussian ruler. The country went through rapid industrialization and soon emerged as the second industrial powerhouse of Europe, after Britain. But the 19th century was ruled by militant German nationalism, which brought about new conflicts and the start of World War I. After the Great War, Germany was devastated, and under the Treaty of Versailles, the new nation-state was forced to accept a humiliating peace. The trauma of war and the humiliation it brought paved the way for the rise of fascism, as discontent with the ruling parties grew due to poverty and overall economic depression. Once Adolf Hitler was appointed as chancellor of Germany, the totalitarian Nazi dictatorship and racist oppression of the Jews and other people groups began.

Hitler's vision of a "Thousand Year Reich" ended after only a decade but left scars on Europe still visible even today. World War II and the genocidal madness of one dictator brought Germany to its knees. After the war, the victorious forces partitioned Germany and paved the way towards the Cold War. While the western parts of Germany managed to exit the post-war crisis with the help of the allied USA, France, and Britain, the eastern parts suffered under the Soviet Union and the iron heel of its leader, Stalin. West Germany returned to democracy, joined NATO, and laid the foundations for the future European Union. But East Germany was a part of the Warsaw Pact and under the strict control of the Soviet Union, which divided it from the west by raising the infamous Berlin Wall. But the communism of the east was doomed to fall, and in 1989 people started demanding changes.

During the peaceful revolution, the government of East Germany fell and opened the way to reunification. With the destruction of the Berlin Wall in 1991, the unification of Germany into the Federate Republic symbolically began. The country was ready to look into the future without being pulled down by the atrocities committed during World War II. Through hard work and cooperation, Germany earned the world's forgiveness and strode proudly forward to become a bastion of liberty and democracy at the front of the European Union.

Chapter 1 – The Early History of Germania

The archeological site which testifies to the earliest history of the region of Germany is the Hohle Fels cave in south Germany (near today's city of Ulm). There, two remarkable facts were discovered. The first is that the first Homo sapiens who migrated to this part of Europe from Africa settled near their genetic cousins, the Neandertals. The second one is that right here, in these caves, humans crafted the first musical instruments. Two flutes that were discovered carbon-dated as far back as 40,000 years. One was made from bird bones and the other from mammoth ivory. What an astonishing discovery! As soon as Homo sapiens came to the regions of today's southern Germany, they started developing art. And music wasn't the only artistic expression our ancestors of the Hohle Fels cave invented. Here the archeologists found some of the earliest examples of human and animal carvings and paintings. It is amazing to think that the first glimpses of culture, music, and art are a part of European heritage! The early humans quickly superseded and replaced the Neanderthals and silently became rulers of the surrounding territories. However, they would not remain the only settlers for long. Other groups of people migrated to the region, and they would all become the settlers of the area we call Germany.

The region today's Germany occupies is geographically unique. It is crossed by three mighty European rivers: the Elbe, Rhine, and Danube. However, it doesn't have natural barriers that would prevent people from migrating or invading. Because of this, a variety of people settled in Germania (the historical name for the region) and called it home. Germania and its history tell us the story of very fluid borders and the constant movement of people. It was only natural that these movements and migrations caused political instability and frequent conflicts. Accordingly, the region of Germania was fragmented, with different cultural and linguistic boundaries, which often changed. The earliest fragmentation we can trace is between Homo sapiens and their neighbors, the Neanderthals. We cannot say if they were ever in open conflict, but their cultures (and probably their languages) differed greatly. While Neanderthals produced crude tools and art, those belonging to Homo sapiens were much more sophisticated. The fragmentation between the two groups wasn't only cultural but also physical. The two peoples were also two different species. However, modern tests show that Neanderthals shared at least 99% of their DNA with Homo sapiens, leading to big questions posed by scholars: did the two species interbreed? Is that how the Neanderthal disappeared? Were they simply absorbed into the genome and culture of Homo sapiens? These questions remain to be answered, and once they are, they will cause many more new questions. This is the beauty of history—it never ends.

The Neanderthals were already long gone (approximately 40,000 years ago) when the Homo sapiens entered the Mesolithic period and roamed central Europe alone. This period began 10,000 years ago, and at that point, humans were a hunter-gatherer society. They remained such for several millennia, but an astonishing change occurred 5,000 to 3,500 years ago. The Homo sapiens of Europe gradually developed the ability to grow crops and produce food.

They also learned how to tame animals and use them for farming, clothing, and food. Because there was no more need to move across central Europe in search of food and game, the humans established the first settled societies of Germania. These early people recognized the value of fertile lands, so the first settlements were built in the wetlands of Northern regions as well as along the banks of the Elbe, Rhine, and Danube. The people settled along other rivers, as well as lakes, but it seems that the first settlements in these locations were seasonal. During warmer days, people took their herds to graze in the fields. Society must have been divided, with some staying in the settlements to work the land around them. The first peoples of central Europe who started their settlements during the Mesolithic and Neolithic period are known to scholars today as the Linear Pottery culture, named after the specific decoration on the pottery they produced. But they weren't the only ones. Later excavations in lower Saxony, at the site known as the Dümmer, discovered a series of settlements ranging from 4,900 to 3,600 BCE. These people are known as the Funnel Beaker culture, and they transitioned from hunting and gathering to farming and herding animals. This specific culture persisted through the Bronze Age until its end (3,200-600 BCE). The Bronze Age saw the rise and fall of many cultures in Germania that worked metal, plowed fields, and grazed livestock. They all displayed different burial rites and included various everyday life items in their tombs, suggesting belief in some kind of afterlife.

The Celts came to the region of Germania sometimes during the Bronze Age and stayed for quite a long time. In fact, their DNA can still be traced in various European peoples from Ireland to the Mediterranean and from Spain to Hungary and even Romania. The Celts were the most influential people in Europe during the Bronze Age. Their origin remains obscure, but some scientific discoveries in their burial practices seem to point to the Urnfield culture as possible ancestors. For example, just like the Celts, people of the Urnfield culture cremated their dead and buried them in urns. The

Urnfield culture disappeared somewhere between 700 and 500 BCE, giving way to several new cultures in Europe, most of them proto-Celtic. The earliest Iron Age civilization that succeeded Urnfield culture was the Hallstatt culture, which flourished between 800 and 450 BCE. They are named for a city in Austria where their culture was first discovered. With the end of Hallstatt culture, Europe saw the rise of another proto-Celtic culture, the La Tène culture. This one was so widespread that it reached Anatolia and Ireland, as well as the central Europe of Germania.

The Celts

The Celts' Expansion in Europe

From these early civilizations, the Celts developed their own culture composed of tribal groups whose society was based on warfare. As such, their aristocracy rose from the military ranks, but the whole group had a reputation for being fierce and warmongering. The classical world is filled with stories about Celtic raids. Romans have probably written the most about the Celts since they suffered the sacking of their city in 390 by the Gauls, who were nothing more than a Celtic group.

Celtic society had a strict class division: warrior elites, druids who practiced religion, and commoners who were pastoral and moved together with their herds. Interestingly, the women of Celtic tribes enjoyed more freedom during the classical era than their Greek or Roman counterparts, who thought of themselves as more civilized than the Celts. The women in Germania could choose their calling and could be warriors, just like men. They could also rule if their predecessor had no male heirs.

Unfortunately, Celts did not leave many written sources, and a large portion of our knowledge about them comes from their contemporaries, the Greeks and the Romans. However, these contemporary civilizations wrote mostly negative comments about the Celtic people since they were victims of their raids and couldn't possibly be objective. The most detailed literary work on Celts comes from a famous Roman military leader, Gaius Julius Caesar. Written between 58 and 50 BCE, the work was named *Commentarii de Bello Gallico,* or *Commentaries on the Gallic War.* (The Celts inhabiting regions of today's France, Luxembourg, and Belgium were named Gauls by Romans who conquered their lands.) But Caesar also led his army through the territory of what is today the German-speaking part of Europe, and he described the people living there. Caesar made a distinction between the Gauls and the Germanic people of central Europe, but his Greek contemporaries thought of them as one people. Culturally, they were similar, but their language was very different. Romans made the classification based on language, and thus the Germanic tribes were born.

Some of the Gaulish tribes were in an alliance with Rome and suffered attacks from Germanic tribes. In one such instance, the tribe known as Aedui, which had allied with Rome, was attacked and defeated by newcomers, the Suebs. Rome was called to aid the Aedui, so consequently, Caesar was the first to describe this new group of people. According to him, the Suebs were a distinct tribe, probably the most aggressive of all Germanic peoples. However, a later Roman historian, Pliny the Elder (1st century AD), thought of them as a larger entity consisting of smaller tribes such as the Lombards, Semnones, and Marcomanni. Another group of Celtic people, the Helvetii, were being pushed from the north by migrating Germanic tribes, and they too fought Romans for their right to inhabit the territory of central Europe. Roman borders were endangered by all these moving tribes of Gauls and Germanic peoples. Caesar decided to protect the borders, and in 58 ADE, he mounted a military expedition to stop Helvetii and Suebi.

A series of conflicts over the years resulted in the expansion of Roman rule. Romans even reached the Northern and Baltic seas of today's northern Germany. In his Commentaries on the Gallic War, Caesar not only described military conflicts and his expedition to conquer Celtic and Germanic tribes but also provided detailed descriptions of the appearance, language, and culture of the peoples he encountered. He noticed similarities in society and culture among the Celtic and Germanic tribes who occupied the regions of Europe that were far away from the Roman influence. These similarities seemed to disappear with closer proximity to Roman territories. Caesar describes Celts and Germanic people of northern Europe as aggressive and fierce, quick to start a quarrel, and hard to fight. He also claims that the Gaul tribes Rome was fighting owed their bravery and valor to the Germanic tribes north of the Rhine with whom they were constantly battling.

The *Commentaries on the Gallic War* could be observed as one of the first ethnographic studies of the Celtic people, especially those living in central Europe. Celts were an enigma to Romans, and the Roman account of these fierce warrior people was biased and filled with negative comments. After all, they were enemies, and Caesar's work is only a fraction of the Roman attitude towards Gauls. For example, Caesar was repulsed by the clan-like structure of Gaul society, which was led by a warrior chieftain who would buy the loyalty of his warband with gifts and lavish feasts.

For Romans, it was the Druidic religion of the Gauls that posed the greatest enigma. Caesar describes Druids as religious leaders and a social class that enjoyed many privileges. Caesar found Druids to be of enormous importance, as one of their tasks was to encourage the battle and inspire valor in the Gaul warriors. Druids never went to war, and it seems they were exempted from paying tribute. Druid religion was oral, so one of their main tasks was to learn the stories and verses they would preserve and pass on to the next generation. Caesar noticed that Gauls used Greek letters for everyday writings, transactions, or public and private messages. However, writing down the Druidic lore was a sacrilege. This is probably because Gauls thought of writing as an inferior method of learning that makes people lazy. Caesar also wrote that Gauls believed in reincarnation and that, because of this, they never feared death. Instead, they were promised that if they died with valor, they would be reborn with a high social rank and many riches.

Pliny the Elder also described Druids in his observations of the religion. According to him, Druids worshiped nature and could read important moments in the future from various natural occurrences, such as stone formations and bird flights. They had no temples but practiced sacred rituals in groves, out in the open. The Druids also sacrificed animals, but in special cases, they would also sacrifice humans. However, no archeological examination confirms the practice of human sacrifice in Celtic society. Nonetheless, it was exactly this that Romans claimed prompted them to ban Druidic practices within the borders of Roman territories in the 2nd century BCE. This ancient Celtic religion died out a century later without leaving any written evidence of its existence.

Caesar's campaign against the Gauls of central and western Europe influenced numerous people groups. The Celts were subjugated to Rome and pacified, and their territories were opened to new migrations of people. It was the Germanic tribes who moved first and inhabited the territory of Germania. They were newcomers here, and they played a dominant role in the history of this region. They not only gave Germany its name but also its culture and language. However, they didn't call themselves Germani. This was a Roman word, probably just a Latin form of an ancient Celtic word that described people similar to themselves but speaking another language.

The Germanic Tribes

At the time of Caesar, the Roman Empire's northern borders were at the Rhine and Danube. But across these waters lived new tribes that posed an even bigger threat than the Gauls. These were the Germanic tribes that migrated from the east—wild, warlike people who wouldn't accept the Roman yoke. Their society was of an egalitarian nature, which Romans couldn't grasp. Fearing the newly-come Germanic tribes, Romans decided to prevent possible future conflicts by invading them. This mission started in the year 12 BCE and was a very small expedition at first. However, Romans soon realized it would take more men and resources to conquer the territories beyond the Rhine, so they sent thousands and thousands of people in the following years. It took them over a decade just to gain the upper hand in the conflict, and three decades after the initial invasion, a decisive battle took place in the Teutoburg Forest (9 CE). But the Germanic tribes were ready, and they united against the common enemy, the Romans. It was the worst defeat Rome experienced since their first endeavors to conquer the tribes of central Europe. The Germanic chieftain who united the tribes against the Romans was Arminius (18 BCE–19 CE). Previously, this chieftain fought in the Roman army as a mercenary. This gave him insight into their tactics and enabled him to plan an ambush and attack, butchering the Roman legions in the woodlands of the Lower Saxony. Roman Emperor Augustus (63 BCE–14 CE) decided to abandon the mission in Germania due to the heavy losses.

But who exactly were these newcomers? Latins would go on to call them *Germani*, but the Germanic peoples never had a common name to unite all the tribes that had migrated to the territory of modern-day Germany during the 1st century BCE. They shared a common language, and this is the main characteristic by which Romans defined them. Modern linguists share the opinion that the

Germanic tribes came from northern Europe but were pushed southward with climate change, which made their homeland hostile to life. The tribes never formed a cohesive group. Instead, they warred among themselves, taking each other's territory, food, women, and riches. Once they arrived in central Europe, their first contact was with the Celts who already occupied the territory. They quickly realized the similarities between their two warlike peoples, but that didn't stop them from fighting for the right to occupy the land. Soon enough, the borders of the Roman Empire were occupied by people who spoke Germanic languages—from Eastern Europe (the Baltic region) to central Europe where today's Germany, Austria, and the Netherlands are, all the way to the British Islands in the northwest.

Germanic people also settled in the western provinces of the Roman Empire, which is today's Belgium and France. However, they were heavily influenced by the Roman culture there and quickly adapted, mingling and assimilating into the local population. Because of this spread out of Germanic tribes across the whole of Europe, Romans were very confused and had difficulty defining them. There were too many different tribes to count, and the Romans simply named them all *Germani.* At first, Romans used the term *Germani* only to refer to the people who lived across the Rhine, but in their inability to describe other peoples who spoke a similar language, Romans soon designated them all the same. It is unknown where this term comes from exactly. The widely accepted proposal is that it is of Celtic origin; however, some linguists suggest an Illyrian or even purely Latin origin. Another term Romans used to unite all the tribes who lived outside their borders and often attacked them was "barbarians." The *Germani* were the barbarians, but not all barbarians were *Germani.* They could also be Celts, Gauls, Illyrians, and later, Slavs. Romans left writings in which they tried to identify and describe different ethnic groups, but they were often in disagreement. Modern scholars find it difficult to discern the truth from ancient Roman texts. Even today, we are unsure which among these diverse people represent distinct ethnic groups or at least a cohesive culture. Roman sources mention different tribes, each having their own names, such as Alemanni, Cimbri, Frisians, Franks, Suebi, and Saxons.

We already learned that Caesar confronted Suebi during his conquest of Gaul and wrote about them, extensively comparing them to the Celts. The main difference between the two groups of people, according to Caesar's observations, was that Germanic tribes gave priority to warfare, praising it above religion and domestic life. Just like the Celtic, the religion of the Germanic tribes was about worshiping nature. However, they had no organized priesthood or Druids to perform various religious rituals. Caesar also describes the pastoral economy of the various tribes that occupied the regions of Germania across the Danube. According to him, the *Germani* were only interested in warfare and raiding as this was how they earned their living. This made them a formidable enemy, unlike more civilized Celtic tribes. He further complained that the Celts were seduced by the luxury of Roman civilization and thus became weak.

Julius Caesar wasn't the only Roman who tried to describe the Germanic peoples. Another Roman aristocrat, born almost 150 years after Caesar, wrote a complete work named *Germania* in 98 CE. His name was Gaius Cornelius Tacitus, and he was born in Roman-ruled Gaul in the year 55 CE. He lived until 120 CE, becoming a politician, consul, senator, and even the governor of Roman provinces in Asia. In addition to his rich career, Tacitus found time to write and describe the peoples who intrigued him the most. Among them were the Germanic peoples, to whom he devoted an entire collection of writings. His intentions were also biased, but unlike Caesar, Tacitus wanted to prove that Romans had become a decadent society compared to brave and virtuous Germanic tribes. Modern scholars are not even sure if Tacitus spent any time on the Roman northern border or if he ever met with the *Germani*, but he did use sources such as Caesar's and Pliny's writings. He probably consulted the Roman merchants and soldiers who encountered the barbarian tribes of central Europe and used their stories to write an ethnographic account named *Germania*.

This work was discovered in the 19th century by German nationalists, who were inspired by Tacitus' description of Germanic valor and bravery. It was Tacitus who was the first to explain Germanic superiority by attributing it to racial purity. He described how Germanic people were untainted by intermarriage with other races and how they were the purest among all peoples known to Romans. However, today it is known that Germanic peoples indeed mixed with other races—for example, the Celts and the Slavs, their immediate neighbors. They also mixed among themselves, and often tribes shared nothing in common except the similarity of their language. Nevertheless, the Germans of the 19th century would start a new nationalistic movement after reading the words of ancient historian and politician Tacitus.

Tacitus' description of Germanic military habits seems more reliable. He wrote that various Germanic tribes, which often fought against each other, would unite on the battlefield when meeting their common enemy, the Romans. The Romans were baffled by this sudden cohesion of the *Germani*, and this was probably the reason they lost so many battles against these barbarians. The *Germani* would choose their common chieftain based on his previous experience and valor on the battlefield. The chieftain had power over his people only as long as he was able to lead them to victory. He would often be demoted after the lost battle and replaced with a more suitable individual. The aristocracy of the Germanic tribes was composed of the best warriors and their immediate families. But no title was hereditary, and each individual had to prove his worth in battle. Tacitus also noticed that, unlike Roman leaders, Germanic chieftains were at the front of the battle lines, not simply giving commands. They were the leaders, and they had to set an example for their followers.

Tacitus also explained the Germanic military success by how their society is structured. He emphasized that Germanic war-bands were composed of family members and clan brethren. Unlike Romans, the Germanic peoples fought next to their kinsmen, which inspired them to show off as well as to watch each other's back. Because proving valor was so deeply engraved in their society, young warriors wanted to prove themselves to their kinsmen and peers, which made them especially dangerous enemies. The bravest warriors were rewarded by chieftains with sizable plunder. Tacitus also explains that they would bring their women and children to the battlefield and fought especially hard to win because they knew their families would be slaughtered or enslaved if they lost. Tacitus believed that the cry of the women and children inspired the Germanic men to fight with vigor and ferocity.

Tacitus also described the wider political and egalitarian nature of the Germanic tribes. He explained that the leaders of different tribes would gather at least once a year to discuss important matters such as warfare, famine, and even birthrates and the exchange of women. While the chieftains had the right to speak first, everyone also had the right to address the assembly and offer insight based on their own experience. The meeting was followed by a lavish feast, where they would all get drunk and celebrate the occasion. These feasts were often ritualistic, symbolizing good fortune and ensuring victory in future battles. But they also served a social function, as such gatherings strengthened the bonds of kinsmen, and many new families would form during the celebrations. According to Tacitus, the Germanic people valued marriage above all and were faithful to their spouses, unlike the decadent Romans of the empire. He insisted that adultery was harshly punished among the Germanic people and that monogamy was highly valued since marriage was considered the strongest bond between two people. Spouses would give gifts to each other on the day of the marriage ceremony, and these gifts included weapons and armor as a symbolic reminder of the primacy of warfare in the Germanic culture.

By the 9th century CE, Romans had conquered some of the territories they designated as Germania. To distinguish it from the area still ruled by the barbaric tribes, they would call the Roman provinces of central Europe *Germania Romana*, while the area beyond the Rhine was named *Germania Barbarica*. The Romans had tried to conquer *Germania Barbarica* continuously since the year 12 BCE but without much success. And when, in 9 CE, Arminius and his warriors ambushed the Roman legion at the Teutoburg Forest, his action was only one small part of the Germanic uprising against the Roman conquest. It was the uprising that convinced Augustus that Germania was not worth invading. The resulting frontier was established at the Rhine-Danube line, known as the Limes Germanicus, and it was held for centuries. However, the peace was uneasy, as the Germanic chieftains demanded payment in exchange for not raiding across the Roman borders. But this static border on the Rhine-Danube line was much more than just a border between the barbarians and the Roman Empire. It was a line that would forever divide the Germanic tribes west of the Rhine, who lived under the Roman rule, and the Germanic tribes in the east. The border also divided their culture, as western Germanic peoples assimilated with Romans and even started using only the Latin language, while the easterners continued their ancient tribal practices and preserved their Germanic language.

During the Roman Empire of Tacitus' time, most of the Germanic tribes settled along the banks of the Rhine and Danube, the territory of today's Germany. Here, the grounds were fertile, and the rivers provided them with life. The border became the site where merchants exchanged their goods and where culture was passed from Rome to Germany and vice versa. Romans founded garrisons along the border, which quickly turned into the towns and later into the culturally-rich German cities of the Middle Ages. Some of these cities exist even today and are known as Trier (Augusta Treverorum), Mainz (Moguntiacum), and Augsburg

(Augusta Vindelicorum). Around the year 300 CE, when Rome was challenged by outside forces, many Germans saw the opportunity to invade, raid, and even to settle in Roman territory. They chose to serve in the Roman army in faraway lands. This service would bring them not only regular pay but also the right to own land within the Roman Empire. Slowly but surely, the Roman world was crumbling, and when the Gauls killed Emperor Valens (328-378) in Thracia, his successor Theodosius (347-395) agreed to cede even more land to keep the peace. But he also had another motive. These Gauls settled at the Rhine-Danube frontier would serve as a buffer from the upcoming Germanic invasion.

By the 5th century, Rome had weakened, and several Germanic tribes, pressured to unite by the constant increase of the population and by the Hunnic invaders, began migrating into the Roman heartland. Visigoths moved towards Greece as the Huns pushed them across the Danube. Their leader, Alaric (370-410), sacked Rome in 410. He then moved his people towards Spain. Another Germanic tribe, the Vandals, moved across Gaul into Spain in 406, and from there crossed to North Africa, which they wrestled from the Roman grip. During these turbulent times, many Germanic chieftains took the opportunity to seize territories that once belonged to the Roman Empire and turn them into their own kingdoms. They completely reorganized Roman administration and subjected the local population to Germanic rule. Germanic kings waged wars against each other, assimilating tribes and consolidating the hold over their new territories. In the 6th century, a new religion appeared among the Germanic tribes, and one by one, the Germanic kingdom succumbed to Arian Christianity. This heterodox sect denied the divinity of Jesus Christ and claimed he was only a human. Because of this, Arian Christianity was declared a sect by the Holy Roman Church at the council of Nicaea in 325.

The scholars of the 18th century thought that the rise of the Germanic tribes was the cause of the Romans' eclipse. However, modern scholars now think that the rise of Germanic tribes was a product of Rome's failing politics. If Rome hadn't weakened due to different influences, Germanic people would never have been able to enter its territories, let alone sack Rome itself. At this point, Germanic people were nothing to be afraid of, and Romans even used them as a force that would defend their outer provinces. They allowed Germanic tribes to inhabit the Roman territories, and more and more Germanic young people showed interest in serving the Roman army. Maybe the Germanic tribes were militarily superior to the Romans at the beginning of the Middle Ages, but Rome played it smart. The emperors, now in Constantinople, were removed from the birthplace of their empire and were even willing to sacrifice it to the incoming barbarians. But they never allowed the Latins to be assimilated. Instead, they managed to turn the Germanic tribes to Roman ideals. Instead of raiding for a living, Germanic kingdoms started growing their own food and producing their own goods. They settled, finally having a territory granted and land they could call their own. And, even though they remained fierce warriors who displayed outstanding bravery on the battlefield, they longed for peace and domesticity in their new homes, where their wives and children waited.

The 6th century saw the previous Western Roman Empire divided into various Germanic kingdoms, which dominated and eventually assimilated the Roman population. Even in Italy, the Germanic kings ruled. The first was Odoacer (433–493), who ruled as a client king of Zeno, Emperor in Constantinople. He was succeeded by Theodoric the Great, a king who is even today seen as one of the mightiest Germanic rulers.

The Franks

Distribution of the Frankish Tribes (green)

During the late 5th century, another Germanic chieftain rose to power, united the tribes which lived between the flow of Lower Rhine and Ems River, and marched on the Roman territory of Gaul. His name was Chlodovocar (466–511), and his people were known as the Franks. Chlodovacar was the first to rule the united Franks instead of numerous chieftains. He is remembered as Clovis, the first king of Franks, who defeated the Roman leader Syagrius in 486 at Soissons. Clovis settled his people in the Roman province of Gaul, absorbing the Roman and Celtic people who already inhabited the area. He married a Burgundian princess, Clotilda, and under her influence, he converted to Roman Catholicism. The baptism of this king remains a famous story, found in *The Chronicles of St. Denis*, where he is described as a pagan who, through a work of miracle and divine intervention, became a Christian.

Clovis turned to Catholicism in 496, and although *The Chronicle* tells a fantastical story of his wife's influence and the inspiration of God, the Frankish king probably had political motives, too. By renouncing paganism, he set an example for the Frankish people, who also accepted Christianity. This way, Clovis had no problem uniting the Franks with the Romans who previously lived in the territory that had become his kingdom. His kingdom now had a united people, bound by the same faith, creating cohesion among the subjects. Other Germanic kingdoms were still pagan and lacked this unity. If they were Christians, Germanic people chose heretical Arian Christianism, which only distanced them from their Roman subjects. Because of this, they were often regarded as foreign or pagan tyrants. Meanwhile, Clovis reaped the benefits of his united people. He quickly became a champion of the faith under the Catholic banner as he slowly started to dominate the other Germanic tribes. Among them were the Thuringians, his mother's tribe, and the dwellers of the Harz Mountains in what would be today's central Germany. He also fought against the Alemanni in 496, but this time his kingdom was invaded. Nevertheless, once he defeated them, he imprisoned their king, Chararic, and his son and took over their territories, which lay near Lake Constance in today's southern Germany.

Clovis was the founder of the Merovingian Dynasty, named after one of his ancestors, probably Merovich. This individual was a part of the Frankish legends, and the connection between the two cannot be confirmed. However, some of the historical sources dating at least a century after the period in which Clovis ruled claim that both Clovis and his Alemanni enemy King Chararic were grandsons of Merovich. Clovis died in 511 and was succeeded by his son Chlotar I. Under him, the Franks conquered even more Germanic tribes and became the rulers of the territory which we today call Germany. They even dared to raid northern lands, where the fierce Saxons lived. These were the territories near the modern region of Holstein.

The Merovingian dynasty started with only one tribe, the Salian Franks. But once they became ardent champions of the Roman Catholic faith, they spread their rule through northern Gaul (modern-day France) and entered central Europe, the territory known as Germania. There, they conquered the Bavarii, Saxons, and Alemanni, adding their territories to the kingdom. The Merovingians ruled until 751, but its kings started leaving the conquest to able military commanders. These commanders had the title Mayor of the Palace and were influential politicians as well as military geniuses. They managed to acquire the right for their sons to inherit the title and start their dynasties of dukes, lords, and princes. The founder of the dynasty which would inherit that position was Charles Martel. He was an illegitimate son of Pepin of Herstal, the Duke and the Prince of the Franks. Charles had to fight for his right to inherit his father's position, and he succeeded in 718. However, once he secured his position as the Mayor of the Palace, Martel became the acting king of the Franks as he controlled and kept Theuderic IV, the Merovingian king, in custody. It would be the son of Charles Martel, Pepin III (the Short), who would usurp the Merovingian throne and start a new dynasty in 751.

With the rise of the Franks and the territorial gains of Clovis, Germania ceased to be the land of the barbarians. The population accepted Christianity, and although in some parts the heretical Arianism lingered, there was no more paganism. Germania became a Christian kingdom, and its kings gained the support of the pope in Rome and the patriarch in Constantinople. The Eastern Roman Empire, better known as the Byzantine Empire, slowly veined and couldn't assert its influence over the newly risen kingdom of the Franks. However, they maintained good relations or chose to simply ignore each other. Even though the kingdom of the Franks was secured, the conflicts never ceased. Internal struggles as well as new neighbors stirred the political situation of Medieval Europe and led it to the new era.

Chapter 2 – The Barbarian Leaders

The ancient history of Germania is complicated. The region was divided between many chieftains, and even though there is evidence they had yearly gatherings to discuss issues pertaining to all the Germanic tribes, they often warred with each other, and the territorial boundaries of their chiefdoms were very fluid. Some lesser tribes were absorbed into the greater ones, leaving little to no trail in history. However, each tribe remained distinctive while gaining a greater sense of belonging to something bigger. The Germani peoples, as Romans used to call them, had a collective awareness and recognized when a common enemy was a threat to their territories. In such cases, they would join forces, showing they were capable of displaying a sense of unity, of a nation, as early as the 2nd century BCE. Perhaps it was the barbaric way of life that divided them and pushed them into conflict with one other. The constant need to show off warrior skills and battle valor, to be recognized by their peers and earn the wealth of plunder, divided them into tribes. Each tribe had its chief, the best among the warriors, one capable of leading his warband into victory. Warfare was a necessity for Germanic tribes—without it, life wouldn't be possible. And warfare would start as soon as the opportunity presented itself.

But when facing an outside enemy, like Rome, the Germanic people would see past their previous quarrels and unite to bring down the threat. The foreign enemy was more than just an opportunity for valor. Romans were invaders who sought not only to add new territory to their enormous empire but also to convert the peoples who already lived there and spoil them with their lavish Roman lives. With their festivities, soft silky clothes, cushioned lives they spent in their marble palaces, the Roman people seemed weak to the barbarians. Romans were effeminate poets and philosophers who only sought to indulge in life's joys. The Germanic people didn't fight only to save their homeland but also to preserve their way of life. During these first conflicts between the Roman Empire and Germanic tribes, some of the greatest barbarian leaders were born. They lived, fought, and died trying to resist the civilized world which lay to the south. Some of them are celebrated even today as if the modern German people have a collective memory of their bravery, courage, and strength.

Arminius (18 BCE–19 CE)

Ancient Rome had a tradition of taking the male offspring of the rulers they defeated as hostages. They would grow up in Rome, directly under the supervision of the emperor. As hostages, these foreign boys weren't imprisoned. Instead, they were given an education, military training, and upbringing equal to that of highborn Romans. Sometimes, they would even study alongside Roman heirs to the throne. One such hostage of Rome was a son of Germanic chieftain Segimerus of the Cherusci tribe. His name is known only in the Latin form: Arminius. His Germanic given name is lost, but today he is known as Hermann throughout Germany.

Arminius was born around 18 or 17 BCE, but it is not known when exactly he was sent to Rome. Once in the capital of the Roman Empire, he received military training and stepped into the service of Rome. It is possible Arminius served alongside Tiberius, the heir of the first Roman emperor, Augustus. The crucial moment for Arminius occurred around the year 8 CE when he was transferred to the Rhine area to fight the Germanic tribes who still resisted becoming Roman provinces. Because of Arminius' Germanic ancestry, he was regarded as a valuable addition to the legions under the service of Publius Quinctilius Varus, who was in charge of pacifying the Germanic tribes in the region. Arminius was even given an auxiliary command, as with this rank he could negotiate with the nobles of the Germanic tribes. But Arminius took the opportunity to re-learn what it meant to be a Germanic man and even reconnected with his family. He met with his father, chieftain Segimer, and together, they planned to get rid of the Roman yoke.

At the time, their tribe, the Cherusci, were already pacified, but Arminius realized the Romans treated them as slaves instead of as part of the foederati (those bound to Rome by a peace treaty) as they were promised. Angered, he agreed to meet with the rest of the Germanic chieftains to make plans for the expulsion of Romans from central Germania. Since he already served the Roman army, he had all the tactical information they needed to devise a successful plan. They were aware that the local Roman garrison was well defended and that they could not attack it and expect victory. Instead, they opted for an ambush in the woods, far away from the fortified walls of the garrison. Arminius' experience in the Roman army won him the allegiance of the Germanic tribes, who united under his command.

The opportunity for the ambush came during the fall when the Roman army decided to move to another garrison on the Rhine for the winter. Arminius already had the support of Germanic tribes such as the Marsi and the Bructeri, but some stubbornly wanted to remain neutral. One such chieftain was Segestes, Armenius' uncle. However, seeing the might of the united armies and their will to fight the Romans, even Segestes joined the rebels, as did many other tribes who were neutral until this point. Of course, some chieftains remained loyal to Rome and even tried to warn Publius

Quinctilius Varus, but he dismissed them, believing they were only jealous of Arminius' privileges since he had grown up in Rome. The attack of the barbarians was so sudden and unexpected that the three Roman legions led by Varus simply dispersed under the rain of arrows and stones which were being thrown at them. Varus tried to restore order, but to no avail. It is believed that Arminius, like a true Germanic leader, was in the middle of the battle, leading the attacks. However, Roman legions were still some of the best-trained armies in the world, and it wasn't an easy task to defeat them. The Romans managed to resist barbarian attacks for three days until, finally, the Germanic tribes overwhelmed them. Varus and the other high-ranking officers chose to commit suicide, as they knew all hope was lost.

The ambush led by Arminius wasn't the end of the Germanic troubles with the Romans. There was still much to do, and in fact, it was only the beginning of a greater uprising. The attacks continued, organized across all of central Germania. Arminius' next target was Aliso, the fort built by Romans on the River Lippe, in the northwestern Rhine area. But he was unable to take the fort until the legions occupying it decided to leave in the middle of the night. The uprising raged on, as the news traveled slowly in ancient times. Once Emperor Augustus received the news of Varus' defeat and the loss of his many legions, he decided the efforts to take Germania were simply not worth it. But the death of the emperor approached, and the conflict in Lower Rhine continued. Germanic tribes still wanted to expel Romans from their territory, and the perfect opportunity presented itself when the Roman legions stationed on the Rhine frontier rebelled against Tiberius' succession to their emperor Augustus.

One person responsible for managing the rebellion was Tiberius' nephew, Germanicus Julius Caesar, the commander of the Rhine frontier. He had to pay the rebellious legionaries to stand down, but sensing that they were still unsatisfied, he managed to channel their anger towards the Germanic tribes who continued attacking them.

At one point, Germanicus and his legionaries confronted Arminius, but instead of defeating him, they only managed to capture his pregnant wife. This enraged the Germanic leader, and he once more called for the unification of the tribes to fight off the invading Romans. The renewed conflict dragged on for years. Some battles were won by the Germanic tribes, others by the Roman legions. It seems that the war against central Germania led to a stalemate, and Emperor Tiberius decided to call off Germanicus and his legions.

Arminius' plan to expel the Romans from central Germania finally succeeded, and he was the leader of the united tribes. He asserted his authority over the tribes, but they refused to name him a king. They still believed in their old system of government: each tribe choosing its own chieftain. Arminius' main challenger at this point was Maroboduus, chieftain of the Marcomanni, who managed to proclaim himself king. Because of this, Maroboduus was hated among his people, and many of them instead joined Arminius. The two Germanic leaders finally met in battle, and Arminius was victorious over the King of Marcomanni, who was forced to run for his life. Arminius now had full authority over the Germanic tribes, but many still denied him the title of king. In 19 CE, tribal warfare occurred, and Arminius was killed in one of the conflicts after his kinsmen betrayed him. The story of his deeds remains thanks to the ancient historian Tacitus, who wrote extensively about this Germanic hero.

Gaiseric (389–477)

In 406, another great migration of the Germanic peoples occurred. In history, it is remembered as the Crossing of the Rhine. Many Germanic tribes who lived in the eastern parts of Germania moved towards the west in search of a better life. The opportunity presented itself as the Western Roman Empire was already veining and the border on the Rhine was weakened. Among the moving tribes were Vandals, led by King Godigisel. But upon their arrival to southwestern Germania, the Vandals came into conflict with the Franks, who killed their king. Godigisel had an illegitimate son,

Gaiseric, who proved his worth and became one of the most powerful men of his tribe. However, he was not their leader—at least not yet. The Vandals' origins are in Scandinavia, but during the 2nd century CE, they migrated to the territory of modern Poland. They continued their migration towards the southwest and eventually reached Spain. There, they were forced into an endless conflict with both the Romans and the Visigoths who occupied the Iberian Peninsula. Gunderic, the legitimate son of ex-king Godigisel, united the Vandals and Alanas and had a large army under his command. However, this army wasn't capable of wrestling Spain out of Roman and Visigoth arms. When Gunderic died in 428 CE, Gaiseric became the king. He was wise enough to see that his people would never prosper in a territory ravaged by eternal conflict. He decided to continue moving and searching for a land where he could establish his kingdom.

The opportunity to seize such land presented itself the same year Gaiseric became the king of Vandals—428. The intrigues of the Byzantine court complicated the situation in the empire. The ruler of the North African province, Boniface, felt threatened by Emperor Valentinian III and his mother, the regent Queen Galla Placidia. To protect himself from possible conflict, he invited the Visigoths to cross the Mediterranean Sea and be his allies against the Byzantine invasion. But this story is only one version of the events. Another story tells of Gaiseric being lame, having injured himself when he fell from a horse. Unable to lead the battle on the land, he wanted to conquer a country by sea, and North Africa was a perfect choice. There is no consensus among historians about how the events played out, but it is quite possible that Gaiseric accepted the invitation from Boniface while planning all along to wait for the opportunity to conquer Carthage.

Around 80,000 Vandals and Alans crossed from Spain into North Africa in 429, invading the Byzantine provinces. It took over fourteen months to take the first city in Africa, Hippo. But once it fell, the Vandals simply overran the rest of the North African territories, from modern-day Morocco to Algeria. Carthage finally fell in 439 CE, and Gaiseric led his army into victory, taking all the cities in North Africa one by one. The court intrigue back in Constantinople further weakened the political scene of the empire, and Emperor Valentinian III had no other choice but to recognize the Vandals as the new rulers of the African provinces. Finally, they had their kingdom. A Germanic tribe had reached the shores of Africa and established a kingdom, which they would rule for a whole century.

Once Gaiseric set his kingdom, the conflict with the Romans didn't simply disappear. It shifted from warfare to religious disagreement—and perhaps disagreement is not a strong enough word. Vandals, just as most Germanic tribes, were Arian Christians, while the Roman Catholics were Trinitarians (believing in the holy trinity of the Father, Son, and Holy Spirit). When Gaiseric took over North Africa, the people he now ruled were a mixture of Vandals and Romans. The hatred between the two was immense, and their king did nothing to prevent it. In fact, he encouraged it by prosecuting the Roman nobility of Africa and even confiscating their lands and possessions. The Roman Catholic populace of his kingdom was taxed heavily compared to the Arians, and he didn't allow Catholics to serve in the government.

Despite the religious conflict within the kingdom, the Vandals in North Africa flourished. They controlled the Mediterranean Sea and built a large fleet. In 442 CE, Gaiseric felt strong enough to lead his men in another conquest. This time, he had Italy in mind. His fleet landed in Ostia, which mounted no defense even though it was aware of the Vandals' approach. The road to Rome was completely opened, and Gaiseric threatened the holy city. Pope Leo I (who served from 440 to 461) negotiated with the Vandal king, and the two came to an agreement that Rome could be sacked if its inhabitants were unharmed and no buildings were destroyed. Gaiseric kept his promise to the pope, and the city was plundered. Among the treasures gathered, Gaiseric found the widow of the late

Byzantian Emperor Valentinian III and took her and her two daughters back to North Africa. The three women remained there for twenty-five years. While Valentinian's wife and younger daughter returned to Constantinople eventually, his eldest daughter, Eudoxia, remained in Africa as the wife of Huneric, son and heir of Gaiseric.

Vandals continued to terrorize the cities of the Mediterranean world, and the Romans were aware they had to deal with them. Even though they never managed to defeat Gaiseric, they eventually managed to end the kingdom of the Vandals. Gaiseric warred openly against the Eastern Roman Empire (the Byzantine Empire) from 469 until 475, but each side had a significant number of victories and losses. Finally, when Zeno became emperor in Constantinople, he sued for peace with the Vandals. He recognized Gaiseric as the king of North Africa and asked in return that the king of the Vandals grant religious freedoms to the Roman people still living there and release all Roman prisoners. Gaiseric agreed to these terms and even promised he would no longer raid the shores of Anatolia and Egypt, which were still Roman provinces. The first Vandal king died of natural causes in 477 and was succeeded by his son, Huneric, who ruled until 484.

No Vandal king ever achieved the same greatness as Gaiseric, and although his kingdom prospered under the rulers who followed, it eventually started to wane. The last king of the Vandals was Gelimer (r. 530–534), who was defeated by Romans in the Battle of Ad Decimum (533). He was taken as a prisoner to Constantinople but was released and given estates in the Roman province of Galatia, where he died of old age. But the Vandals of North Africa ceased to be a nation, a cultural entity. They were absorbed into the Roman Empire and assimilated into the Roman way of life.

Odoacer (431–493)

As we saw in the example of Gaiseric, not all famous Germanic leaders ruled Germanic lands. Those who are remembered as heroes and great kings were usually conquerors, and they became famous for ruling foreign lands. Another stellar example of a Germanic leader is Odoacer, the first king of Italy. Although his ethnicity is disputed, the consensus among scholars is that he is of Germanic descent. Nothing is known of Odoacer's youth, and history can't pinpoint his birthplace, but it is possible he was the son of Edico (or Edeko) of the Germanic Sciri tribe. If this is true, Odoacer was the son of the great adviser of Attila the Hun. Unfortunately, there are three Edicos known to history, and they were all contemporaries. It is impossible to conclude which one was Odoacer's father.

The first mention of Odoacer in history is legendary. The *Life of Saint Severinus* by Eugippius, dated to the 5th century CE, tells the story of a soldier named Odoacer who found the saint in his home and asked for a blessing. Saint Severinus prophetically told him to go to Italy, as that is where he would find riches. Young Odoacer listened to the saint and stepped into the service of the Roman army. By 470, he rose to the rank of an officer and served under the military commander Orestes. Odoacer witnessed when Orestes overthrew the Western Roman Emperor Julius Nepos and placed his son on the throne. He might even have helped the commander, as Orestes had the full support of the Roman army. But then the army asked Orestes for payment in the form of a land they could settle and call home. They asked for a third of Italy's territory, and the new emperor and his father, Orestes, hesitated to answer—only because that territory was already settled. Expelling the Roman citizens from their homes would mean a certain rebellion and condemnation from the emperor of Constantinople, who was already against their rule.

Orestes didn't count on the ambitions of his officer of Germanic origin, Odoacer. He gathered the angry soldiers around him and promised that if they followed him into rebellion, they would be properly compensated. Together with what was left of the Roman army, Orestes fled to the city of Pavia to mount a defense, as he knew Odoacer was coming for him. But he didn't linger there, as it seemed that Odoacer would easily take Pavia. So, Orestes decided to reorganize his army at Piacenza, where the decisive battle occurred. Odoacer defeated Orestes and executed him. The soldiers elevated their new leader to the position of king. However, he yet had to deal with Emperor Romulus, son of Orestes. Another battle was fought at Ravenna on September 2, 476, in which the emperor was deposed. Orestes refused to kill Romulus; instead, he exiled him from Italy. From this point, all traces of Romulus Augustus disappear. Although Odoacer was proclaimed a king of Italy, he never strived for independence. Instead, he ruled as a subject of Emperor Zeno in Constantinople.

As a new king, Odoacer couldn't simply begin his rule. The old emperor, Nepos, still claimed the right to the throne of the Western Roman Empire, even though he was hiding in his villa in Dalmatia. Odoacer never moved directly against Nepos, but the old emperor was assassinated in his home in 480, which allowed Odoacer to annex Dalmatia. He also made a treaty with the Vandals and, through it, acquired Sicily. It is unknown how he solved the problem of the army that demanded one third of Italian territory as their property, but during his rule, he was admired by his soldiers, and they never showed anything but loyalty. The Roman senate still functioned throughout the reign of Odoacer, and it gave the new king its support. Because of this, or maybe influenced by the senate, Odoacer ruled as a Roman king, not a Barbarian. He even adopted the Roman name Flavius and added it to his birth name Odoacer. Even though he was an Aryan Christian just like other Germanic leaders, it seems that his kingdom was filled with religious tolerance, as there is no evidence of special taxes enforced on Roman Christians. The Roman Christian sources dating to the rule of Odoacer do not contain any complaints about his rule.

Odoacer's annexation of Dalmatia bothered Zeno, who saw it as the clear sign that the Italian king was trying to rule independently. The conflict between the king and the emperor in Constantinople deepened once Odoacer agreed to fight on the side of the anti-Zeno party in the Middle East. The emperor saw this as a direct threat to his own rule and made an agreement with Theodoric of the Goths, who was to dispose of Odoacer and rule Italy in Zeno's name. However, this proved to be a very difficult task. Theodoric was unable to defeat the Italian army, but his persistence in the conquest led to a joint rule. It was the Bishop of Ravenna who mediated the treaty between Odoacer and Theodoric until they both agreed to split the rule of Italy. However, during the celebration ceremony in honor of the treaty, Theodoric stabbed Odoacer to death and proclaimed himself sole ruler.

Odoacer was a very pious ruler, and he set it as his goal to preserve Roman nature, ideals, and culture throughout his reign. It is quite possible that if he decided to be as Barbarian as his contemporaries saw him, Italy would never transform into a medieval culture. Perhaps even the Renaissance would have been delayed. The Roman Empire was already entering its eclipse, and if not for people like Odoacer, who saw the value of its tradition, it would certainly have fallen much earlier. Even if only for one generation, Rome survived the hard times of early medieval history. But it would take another Germanic ruler to complete the transformation of the Italian peninsula, and he would create a kingdom of Italy completely independent of its Byzantine imprisonment. This Germanic ruler of Italy was greatly respected by his contemporaries and quickly became known as Theodoric the Great.

Clovis I (466-513)

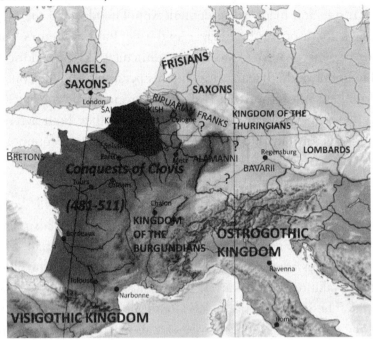

The Conquests of Clovis until 511

Clovis I was only fifteen years old when his father died and he assumed the throne of the Salian Franks. This tribe came to prominence as they fought against the invading Huns, on the side of the Romans. Even though he was so young, Clovis was well prepared for rule and quickly asserted his dominion over the other pretenders to the throne. By the age of twenty, he was already commanding an army large enough to oppose the governor of Roman Gaul, Syagrius. The Franks were not yet united under a single rule, but Clovis realized the importance of family alliances and asked his cousins Ragnachar and Chararic, petty kings of other Frankish tribes, for help against the Roman commander. While the first one accepted the alliance, the latter one refused. Chararic wanted to remain neutral during the conflict with Rome and decided later to join the winning side. But Clovis didn't want his cousin to be such an open threat, so, instead of marching against

Rome, he turned against Chararic. Clovis managed to win the conflict and imprison his cousin. Later, Clovis had him executed and his petty kingdom annexed.

When he finally turned towards the Romans in 486, the Battle of Soissons occurred, and Clovis defeated Syagrius, who fled to Toulouse to seek shelter in the court of the Visigoth King Alaric II. Alaric refused to meddle in the conflict and refused Syagrius, allowing Clovis to capture and execute the Roman general. Clovis continued the conquest of Roman Gaul, and one by one, the cities of Reims, Rouen, and Paris fell under his command. He even killed Ragnachar, his cousin and ally, just so he could annex his petty kingdom, too. By 495, Clovis extended his dominion throughout western Gaul and finally conquered it entirely when he fought against the Alemani, pushing them across the Rhine River in 506. Almost the whole region of today's France was under the rule of Clovis I. Once he converted to Christianity, he found religious reasons to fight the Visigoths and push them across the Pyrenees into Spain. Christianity also brought recognition from the Eastern Roman Empire because, unlike other Germanic leaders, Clovis refused Arianism and converted to Catholicism. He shared the religion of the Byzantine Emperor Anastasius, who offered him an alliance.

The final battle with the Visigoths occurred in 507 when Clovis killed their king, Alaric II, at the Battle of Vouille. Even though the Visigoths had allied with the king of Italy, Theodoric the Great, it was the alliance between Clovis and the Byzantine Emperor Anastasius that prevailed. Since Constantinople had allowed Theodoric to rise to power in the first place, Anastasius vetoed him from meddling in the conflict between the Franks and the Visigoths. Alaric II was on his own against the might of the united Franks, and even though he fought vigorously, he didn't manage to save his kingdom. Once Clovis expelled the Visigoths from Frankia, he received the "royal purple" from Anastasius and chose Paris as his capital. But he didn't manage to take all the territories previously ruled by Alaric, as Theodoric the Great claimed Provence for his grandson. Theodoric had married one of his daughters to Alaric II, and through their marriage and offspring, he asserted his right to this territory.

Clovis I died in November of either 511 or 513—historians can't seem to agree on the exact year. His kingdom was a mixture of Roman and Germanic culture and language as well as faith. While most of the Roman populace were Catholics, the Germanic part remained Aryan Christian even though their king renounced this religion. Nevertheless, the kingdom functioned as united peoples tolerated each other. With the death of Clovis I came the end of the Frankish expansion. The kingdom was already large, having taken the territories of Alemanni, Burgundians, Visigoths, and absorbing the smaller Frankish kingdoms which once occupied today's France. But all these territories were divided again between Clovis' four sons. While their father became regarded as the founder of modern-day France, their reigns were uneventful. Clovis was a Germanic name, but it was Latinized by early historians and changed to Louis, a name that would persist in the history of France. Eighteen kings named Louis would rule these territories for centuries to come.

Chapter 3 – The Merovingians and the Carolingians

After the death of Clovis, the kingdom was divided: first between his four sons and then again between his grandsons. The territory of Frankia continued to be partitioned with the passing of each of its subsequent kings. The throne pretenders often fought each other for supremacy, hoping to add their cousins' kingdoms to their own. For almost 150 years, the Merovingians ruled small kingdoms of Frankia without the desire to unite, expand, or better the lives of their subjects. They returned to their tribal instincts, with each family fighting for its own right to rule. This stage of unrest in Frankia lasted until 613, when Clotar II dared to dream of unification once more.

At first, Clothar ruled a very small kingdom called Neustria, located to the west of Frankia. Even though it was territorially small, Neustria was rich because it incorporated important trade centers and the cities of Paris and Orleans. But soon, it was reduced to the regions covering only Rouen, Beauvais, and Amiens. Clothar attempted to regain his kingdom on several occasions. The first was disastrous, but with each effort, he would take cities one by one. Realizing his worth, many of Clothar's cousins asked for his support in various dynastic conflicts that occurred after the death of the Merovingian kings of various territories. These were times of unusual instability in which families couldn't agree who should rule what. Court plots often resulted in the murder of children, potential wives of kings and their heirs, and even the kings themselves. The assassination of male children occurred so often that many ruling families resorted to raising them in secrecy. Clothar survived only because he was raised in a private villa, under the watchful eyes of loyal servants.

Clothar never shied away from plots and dynastic conflicts, which were regarded as normal at the time. Some historians see them as the barbarian heritage of the Franks from past times when, through conflict, various individuals had to prove they were worthy of rule. Clothar allied with his cousin Theuderic, ruler of Austrasia, but once Theuderic died in 613, he turned against his successor, Sigebert II. But it was the Austrasian nobles who abandoned Sigebert in favor of Clothar, and by deserting their rightful king, they handed Frankia to Clothar. With his previous conflicts against other cousins and kings, Clothar became the sole ruler of Frankia. The land was once more united, at least for some time. Unfortunately, history repeated itself after the death of Clothar's son Dagobert I, and the kingdom was again partitioned.

Dagobert is the last Merovingian king who was strong enough to hold the kingdom under one rule. It is believed that his successors had no real executive powers, as they allowed kingdoms to fall under the rule of palace mayors. Even though the internal conflict within Frankia was tearing the country apart, Merovingian kingdoms still fought some of the Germanic tribes of central Europe. At its prime, Frankia wasn't only modern-day France. It also incorporated the territories of modern Germany. In the north, it stretched almost to the banks of the Baltic Sea, but this was still the territory of the Saxons. The Upper Rhine, together with cities such as Cologne and Meinz (in modern Germany), was a part of the Frankish kingdom. Although the Saxons, Alemanni, and Bavarians frequently warred with the Frankish kingdom, their territories were never annexed. Instead, they were turned into tributary states. During the 6th century, Frankia became the largest empire in Europe. But during the 7th and 8th centuries, the country saw more dynastic wars as the various mayors of the palace fought for supremacy. "King" became nothing more than a ceremonial title, while these mayors had all the real power. Through military conflict, they usurped each other's territories, and it wasn't unusual for close cousins to fight. With the rise of Charles Martel, a new era was dawning: the Carolingian Empire.

The Carolingian Dynasty

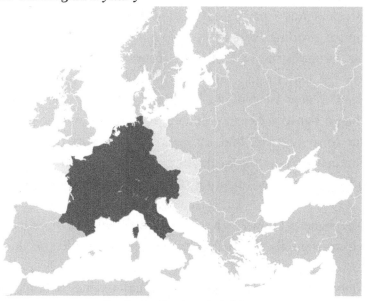

Carolingian Empire at its height
Blank map of Europe.svg: maix_C?derivative work: Alphathon, CC BY-SA 4.0 <https://creativecommons.org/licenses/by-sa/4.0>, via Wikimedia Commons https://commons.wikimedia.org/wiki/File:Francia_814.svg

Charles Martel was never officially a king but acted as one beginning in 737 when King Theuderic IV of the Merovingian dynasty died. However, he worked aggressively to secure the Frankish throne for his sons. Since they were not of the Merovingian dynasty, Charles Martel had to gain the proper titles for himself and his children. Through various political and military accomplishments, he was awarded the title of prince, and as such, he ruled until he died in 741. At that point, no one was politically strong enough to deny his sons, Pepin and Carloman, the right to succeed the throne of the Frankish Empire. As tradition commanded, the empire was split once more. Carloman was proclaimed ruler of the eastern part, which included Alamannia, Bavaria, Thuringia, and Austrasia (most of today's Germany), while the western part of the empire, which included Burgundy, Provence, and Neustria (most of today's France), was ruled by Pepin.

The greatest member of the Carolingian dynasty and one of the early rulers was Charlemagne (742-814). The early Carolingians continued dividing the empire among their heirs, and the internal power struggles never stopped. However, once Pope Leo III crowned Charlemagne emperor in 800, the Frankish dynasty adopted a new view of their empire. Although the tradition of dividing it between heirs continued, the empire was now seen as a higher form of state, and as such, it needed to remain unified. Contradicting views on the Frankish Empire continued, and while its rulers made their offspring rulers of little kingdoms, they were still a part of the larger entity, the empire. In Germany, Charlemagne is known as Karl der Grosse, and he played a pivotal role in forming the Germanic Empire, which would rise under his successors.

Traditionally, the coronation of Charlemagne as emperor was seen as the birth of the Holy Roman Empire. But newer research suggests that the idea of the Holy Roman Empire was only being developed during his reign. He was simply seen as the Western emperor who opposed the Eastern emperor in Constantinople. Modern scholars now agree that the Holy Roman Empire is a creation of later times, but they do not dispute the significance of Charlemagne. He was, after all, the ruler who shaped the society of Europe and what would become the German Empire.

Charlemagne understood that his coronation as emperor was an attempt to continue the Western Roman Empire, which had fallen centuries ago. To honor the pope's wishes, he styled his empire as the ancient Roman emperors did before him, but he couldn't simply adopt new values and force them onto his subjects. Instead, he created a mixture of Roman administration, Christian piousness, and Germanic military power. These three elements of Charlemagne's empire would later be the foundation on which German society would be raised. But Charlemagne wasn't only a Roman emperor. He was also a devout Christian who pleased the pope. In the name of religion, as well as to expand the borders of his empire, Charlemagne fought the pagan people beyond his borders: Saxons, Slavs, and the Avars. Of all the tribes, Saxons were the thorn of Germanic-ruled Europe. They were a Germanic tribe, relatives of the Franks, and Charlemagne desperately wanted to integrate them into his empire. The main problem for the emperor was that Saxons were the last of the Germanic tribes to linger in their pagan religion, and although they promised they would convert and stop plundering the Frankish territories beyond the Rhine, they broke their promise as soon as Charlemagne's attention was elsewhere. It took a series of military expeditions from 772 to 804 (known as the Saxon Wars) for Charlemagne to defeat them, Christianize them, and integrate them into his empire.

The Roman influence on Charlemagne's empire can be seen in the appointment of governors, or consuls, who had the task of administering specific regions. The only difference was in the name of these administrators, as they were renamed counts. To keep the counts in check, Charlemagne employed imperial officials who would travel the vast empire to enforce the royal decrees. They were equal in power to the counts or even slightly above them, but their titles weren't hereditary, so they had no reason to gather power. Most of the royal officials serving the empire were monks and priests because they were the only literate social group within the empire. While nobles could afford tutors to teach them how to read and write, literacy was mostly confined to the church. Charlemagne himself usually spent his time on the battlefield, though he did hold courts in various cities around his empire. He never had a capital, but some of the cities were more significant than others. In Germania during the 800s, it was Aachen which became the center of Latin scholarship and culture. Charlemagne probably favored this city, as he founded its cathedral and spent most of the winters here. The city soon became the political center of the empire, and when Charlemagne died in 814, he was buried there.

The tradition of dynastical power struggles continued after the death of Charlemagne, and his successors, once again, turned to the partition of the empire. Because the Frankish rule was that all male successors inherited a part of the patrimony, Charlemagne made a decree in 806 by which his empire would be split among his three sons. Fortunately, only one son managed to outlive his father, Louis the Pious (774-840). In 814, he became emperor, and the Carolingian empire remained whole for another generation. But during Louis' reign, his own three sons warred among themselves, each wanting to secure his right to rule after the death of Emperor Louis the Pious. His sons were Charles the Bald (823-877), Louis the German (804-876), and Lothair (795-855). The three brothers made peace in 843 with the Treaty of Verdun. The empire was divided into the western part ruled by Charles the Bald (roughly modern France and Belgium), a middle part known as Lotharingia ruled by Lothair (central Europe from the North Sea to Italy), and an eastern part known as East Francia ruled by Louis the German (all the lands of the Carolingian Empire east of the Rhine).

When Lothair died, fifteen years of interregnum followed. Then, in 870, the two remaining brothers split Lotharingia between themselves. But only a decade later, after the death of Charles the Bald, Louis the German invaded his brother's part of Lotharingia and integrated it into East Frankia with a status of a dutchy. This territory would remain a disputed land and the cause of many wars between Francia and Germania over the next 1,000 years. But it is the death of Louis the Pious in 840 which marks the split of the Carolingian Empire into France and Germany. In the western part, people spoke medieval Latin, from which the French language would be born. But in the east, where people weren't as much under Roman influence, the spoken language was Germanic, which would later develop into modern German. Louis the German and his successors ruled as direct descendants of Charlemagne, and as such, they held the imperial title. The German-speaking continuation of the Carolingian Empire occupied central Europe and would soon develop into the Holy Roman Empire. With the first Holy Roman Emperor, Otto the Great, the basis for the German identity was born.

Chapter 4 – The Holy Roman Empire

The old Germanic territories started becoming a powerful central European kingdom in 936 with the coronation of Otto I as the king of the Germans. Throughout his reign, Otto established himself as a formidable ruler by defeating the Magyars, conquering territories that belonged to the Slavs beyond the Elbe river, and skillfully maneuvering his political allies and rivals. Otto's journey eventually led him to be crowned as the first Holy Roman Emperor in 962.

Otto's coronation took place in Rome, and thus began the millennia-long German ownership of the imperial title. The Holy Roman Empire is the anvil on which the German identity was forged. It united all the Germanic tribes in what we know today as Germany and was the foundation of a new major power in Europe.

The Dynasty Genealogy found in a 13th-century manuscript
https://commons.wikimedia.org/wiki/File:StammtafelOttonen0002.jpg

With the death of Charlemagne in 814, the Carolingian Empire began to slowly crumble. This signaled the end of Frankish dominion and launched the separate evolution of what we call Germany and France. Charlemagne's empire continued briefly under the control of his son, Louis the Pious, but after his death, the members of the dynasty fought a civil war lasting for three years. The empire finally broke apart at the end of the war with the signing of the Treaty of Verdun.

The Carolingian Empire was no more, and the states that rose from its ashes had to defend themselves on their own. One of these states was East Francia, a land ruled by several Germanic peoples, such as the Saxons, Bavarians, and the Franconians. They were the descendants of the ancient tribes and warbands that had dominated those territories from Roman times. But East Francia, broken away from the Carolingian Empire, was now being attacked from all sides by foreign invaders. The most notable ones were the Vikings who came from the north, raiding the border by sea, and the Magyars who attacked from the east.

The new Germanic kingdom was unstable. In 911, the remnants of the Carolingian dynasty faded out in East Francia, replaced by local noblemen. These new administrators proved to be highly ineffective and incompetent, so they requested help from the House of Saxony. Interestingly, just a century earlier, the Saxons were pagans and enemies of the Carolingians, but they were about to become a significant power and a driving force inside East Francia.

The Frankian dukes had elected Henry I, nicknamed "the Fowler," to be crowned in 919 as king of the Germans. This event marks the beginning of the Ottonian dynasty. Henry's first major act as king was to form a bond of vassalage with the Bavarian, Saxon, Swabian, and Franconian lords. This meant that the noblemen declared their allegiance to Henry but were still allowed to rule their tribes and peoples.

The German feudal alliance was first tested in 933 when Henry gathered an army composed of multiple Germanic tribes that were part of East Francia. The purpose of the army was to push against the Magyars who were consistently raiding the eastern borders. Henry emerged victorious and pressed on to vanquish the Danes who were invading Frisia. Henry proved to be a skilled military and political leader, having successfully gathered people from different tribes and marched them into battle against foreign invaders. His campaigns solidified his rule and the support he received from the noblemen.

Henry I forged the system that would govern the Holy Roman Empire over the next few centuries. He believed in a decentralized governing structure, thus allowing the lords of the five great

Germanic houses—Franconia, Saxony, Bavaria, Swabia, and Lotharingia—to keep their autonomy and rule their own tribes. He even had plans to organize an expedition to Rome to receive the title of emperor from the pope. However, in 936, the king of the Germans died unexpectedly. But Henry's crown didn't automatically pass to his heir. After all, he was an elected figure. At the time, the king had to be elected by the dukes of the great houses. And so, they did. The dukes were pleased with Henry's rule and with the fact that he allowed them to govern and administer their lands and people, so they voted for Otto, Henry's son, to become the next king of the Germans.

Otto was crowned in 936 in Aachen, and documents from that period show that he was named "Otto I, Theutonicorum rex," which translates to "Otto the First, king of the Germans." He was an ambitious ruler that walked in his father's path, but he wanted to reach a further goal. Otto quickly demonstrated he was a capable leader on the battlefield by defeating the Magyar nomads and reinforcing the eastern borders. He didn't stop there, as he launched multiple military campaigns against the Slavic tribes that dominated between the Elbe and the Oder rivers. His conquest against the Slavs was successful, but he didn't stop at enforcing his rule over them. Otto assigned Christian bishops to convert the pagan Slavs to Christianity. He did the same once he conquered the Danes and the Bohemians, as well.

Otto used the Roman Catholic faith to unite the different tribes under his rule. The Ottonian dynasty now held a solid foothold by exerting control over not only the German dukes but also the non-Germanic tribes, and by investing in capable bishops. His campaigns brought new lands and peoples under Francian dominion.

Otto I reached the height of his power in 962 by doing what his father set out to do before his life was suddenly cut short: he traveled to Rome to help the pope end a dispute in Lombardy and, as a reward, claimed the title of emperor. There he was anointed in

Saint Peter's Basilica as the Holy Roman Emperor. The title was finally renewed after being left unclaimed for almost forty years. This act reinforced the noble status of German rule by reminding people of Charlemagne and reconstructing the old Frankish alliance with Rome.

Otto's coronation would lead to the imperial tradition of all German rulers receiving the prestigious title in the centuries that followed. However, despite being coronated as emperor, Otto did not have the authority to directly control all the other Germanic tribes. Their dukes still held autonomy, even though they were bound to serve the emperor. But this didn't stop Otto from doing everything in his power to assert his royal dominion. Unfortunately, Germany as a unified state remained a dream. When Otto I died in 973, the German tribes were more united under the royal authority than ever before; however, that didn't last.

With Otto's death, his descendants had to pacify multiple rebellions organized by some of the noblemen, as well as foreign invaders. In the following decades, the Ottonian dynasty spent much of its power, influence, and resources on holding together everything that Henry and Otto had built. However, despite remarkable efforts and strong leadership, Otto's imperial lineage ended with Henry II in 1024 due to a lack of heirs.

The Salian Dynasty

The end of the Ottonian dynasty marked the beginning of a new chapter in Germanic history. Henry II's death caused a power vacuum and, with it, a significant amount of internal turmoil. However, the dukes of the Germanic tribes came to a solution by electing Conrad II as the new Holy Roman Emperor. He would be the first of Franconian noblemen to take the crown of overlordship. The Salian dynasty was born.

After Henry's death, a century of the Salian rule followed, marked by four emperors who would turn the newly built Holy Roman Empire into one of the most significant powers on the European continent. The Salian dynasty continued many of the political and administrative policies instituted by the Ottonian rulers, but it also launched the process of centralization. Administration of the empire was centralized under imperial authority partially to subdue the dukes that had rebelled after Otto's death. To achieve this goal, the Salian emperors sought to use the alliance with the pope because it brought influence, power, and prestige.

Conrad II was crowned emperor in 1027, and a solid alliance was formed with the papacy. But that would later change when in 1075, the pope began a campaign of dominance over the ancient lands of the German tribes. During the time of the Ottonians, the relationship between the German administration and the Catholic Church was symbiotic. The two cooperated, and the Holy Roman Emperors acted as important leaders and protectors of Christendom. However, the papacy wanted to break the separation between state and church and therefore launched a campaign of reforms. One of the most significant events occurred when Pope Gregory VII issued an order for Emperor Henry IV of the Salian dynasty to give up his right to choose his bishops. At the same time, the papacy also issued a decree that banned any Catholic Church official from accepting a position appointed by a secular ruler.

This posed a major problem for the Salian dynasty—and the imperial rule, in general. The bishops weren't just representatives of the Church that spread Christianity throughout the land. They also acted as local administrators and owned land. But Henry IV refused to relinquish his right and sent a stern letter to the pope, accusing him of being hungry for power and trying to usurp what didn't belong to him. Henry's letter angered Pope Gregory. The conflict between the two figures escalated so much that the pope excommunicated Henry and forbade members of the church, as well as any vassals, from accepting appointments and orders from the emperor.

The pope's actions gave the German nobles the opportunity to rebel against the imperial crown once again. To stop that from happening, Henry arranged for an expedition in 1077 into the Italian Alps, where he spent several days waiting for Pope Gregory to grant him an audience. The emperor spent that time on his knees, despite the snow, forcing the pope's hand to receive him. His appearance as a humble man repenting for his crimes and begging for forgiveness from the church pushed the pope's hand to absolve him. As soon as Henry ended the conflict with Pope Gregory, he started appointing new bishops that would support him and even went as far as setting up a new papal election by supporting one of Gregory's rivals.

While Henry was successful in partially de-escalating his conflict with the pope, the situation back home didn't improve. In fact, during the next several decades, the noblemen led a long campaign against the emperor. It was the year 1122 when the rebellion ended, but no side emerged victoriously. An agreement called the Concordat of Worms was signed, giving the pope the power to name the bishops in the Holy Roman Empire. However, the emperor would retain veto power. But the conflict had also led to several changes that diminished the imperial crown's power. Further decentralization reduced the powers and rights of the emperor and thus diminished the direct control he held over the German peoples and their territories. This is a key factor that would continue to influence the Holy Roman Empire until its end.

The political and religious changes didn't affect just the papacy and the German nobility. The common people who lived during the 11th century, as well as the following century, felt the effects as well. The most revolutionary change was the rapid expansion of cities and the urbanization of many areas. This alone boosted the economy significantly. However, it was also promoted and funded thanks to the trade provided by the ongoing crusades during that time. Many new free cities were founded, while others claimed municipal liberty. These free cities were essentially free from serving the noblemen and the dukes, as they only had to swear loyalty to the emperor. Trade brought wealth, and many merchants and skilled traders moved to the free cities. They gradually formed guilds (associations), and as their economic power grew, so did their control over the markets and cities.

Guilds became the main force that drove the economy and pushed education further. Long-distance trading, whether by land or sea, increased greatly during the period between the 11th and 14th centuries. Some of the guilds from northern German cities banded together to form the Hanseatic League, a trade alliance that controlled most of the trade and shipping on the northern coast of Germany as well as the North Sea and Baltic Sea. At the same time, various German peoples expanded and settled in the regions that used to be dominated by the Slavs, such as Silesia and Bohemia.

The Hohenstaufen Dynasty

The Holy Roman Empire at its peak under the rule of the Hohenstaufen
Alphathon /ˈælfə.θɒn/, CC BY-SA 4.0 <https://creativecommons.org/licenses/by-sa/4.0>,
via Wikimedia Commons
https://commons.wikimedia.org/wiki/File:Mitteleuropa_zur_Zeit_der_Staufer.svg

The Salian imperial dynasty remained at the helm of the Holy Roman Empire until 1125, when the last Salian Emperor, Henry V, died from an illness. He had no heirs of his own. Henry named his nephew, Frederick II, as heir to his titles and possessions. With the death of the emperor, the nobles of the great German houses prepared for a new election. Frederick II of Hohenstaufen was the main candidate because he was the closest relation to Henry V. However, Frederick was arrogant and believed he could win the imperial title without compromising with the German princes. An election was held, but Frederick II was overconfident and refused to grant the princes the right to elect whether he would be emperor. The nobles did not want to return to an autocratic form of government that relied on familial succession, so they denied Frederick the title.

Several other candidates were available, but the elections did not continue smoothly. The imperial claimants were rivals and launched violent campaigns against each other. It took almost three decades after Henry V's death for stability to be reestablished when Frederick I of Swabia, a member of the Hohenstaufen lineage, victoriously navigated through the political conflicts. Also referred to as Frederick Barbarossa due to his ginger beard, he became the newly elected emperor of the Holy Roman Empire in 1152 (crowned by the Pope in 1155) and enjoyed a long reign until 1190.

Frederick I focused on restoring the rights and power of the crown as they were during Emperor Otto I's times. Due to the gradual decentralization that was supported by the great nobles, as well as the compromises made with the papacy during the Salian administration, the emperor had become almost powerless. The title was more of a symbol than actual authority. The heads of the noble houses ruled over their own lands, just like kings did. Besides, they no longer offered financial and military support to their emperor as they had during Ottonian dominance. This forced the emperor to use his own family's resources and whatever his territory could provide.

Frederick Barbarossa wanted to return power to the imperial crown. To achieve this, he organized multiple expeditions into Northern Italy, which was part of the empire, hoping to use some of its resources to improve his position in the German territories. During his first expedition in 1155, he helped the papacy quell a rebellion in Rome, thus improving the crown's relations with the pope, and was ceremonially crowned in Rome. However, his activity in Italy wasn't the only thing that occupied his time. He was also involved with the crusades.

In 1188, Jerusalem fell to Saladin's army. During that same year, the Diet of Mainz was held, where Frederick Barbarossa swore in front of the empire's Estates General to join the campaigns in the Holy Land. In 1189, the emperor joined Richard the Lionheart (the English) and Philip Augustus (the French) in a military campaign, known as the Third Crusade or King's Crusade, to retake control of Jerusalem. The combined forces were victorious against all odds, even though they were smaller in number than Saladin's army.

However, this victory didn't last long for Frederick because, on June 10, 1190, he drowned in the Saleph River during the campaign for Antioch. With the death of the emperor, the imperial troops lacked order and leadership and were easily defeated by the enemy. Only a small number of his forces survived and retreated to the crusader city of Acre. The military campaign ended as a disaster for the Holy Roman Empire. However, Frederick Barbarossa became a legendary figure as stories were told about him in the empire for generations. One of the most famous myths says that the emperor did not die in battle but lies asleep under the Kyffhäuser Mountains, located in the modern-day German state of Thuringia. There he waits for a time when the German people are in their hour of greatest need, to rise and lead them to greatness.

With the death of Frederick I, his son Henry IV took the imperial crown. His reign was short, lasting from 1190 to 1197. He focused on his father's affairs in Italy, and with his absence in Germany, the nobles began spreading their influence by ignoring the emperor's authority. Instability was once again present in the Holy Roman Empire, and it only worsened with the death of Henry IV. The internal struggle for dominance continued until 1215, when a new emperor rose to power, namely Frederick II. He took control over the empire, ruling for thirty-five years.

Just like the other Hohenstaufen emperors before him, Frederick II focused his attention on Italy, fighting against the papacy. And just like before, the German nobles were plotting to spread their control and dominance over imperial territories. But

Frederick II was successful in bribing them by giving up some of his authority in exchange for stability and peace. The emperor gained support from the princes by offering them nearly complete autonomy over their states. Despite the brief respite, once the emperor's heir, Conrad IV, died, the nobles started producing new claimants for the imperial title. These actions led to another period of uncertainty and instability in the empire. During the following decades, the emperor lost most of his authority once again as the German noble families succeeded in taking full control over their lands.

The Black Death in the Holy Roman Empire

1346 1347 1348 1349 1350 1351 1352 1353

- - - Approximate border between the Principality of Kiev and the Golden Horde - passage prohibited for Christians.

🖜 Land trade routes

🖜 Maritime trade routes

The spread of the black plague in Europe

Flappiefh, CC BY-SA 4.0 <https://creativecommons.org/licenses/by-sa/4.0>, via Wikimedia Commons https://commons.wikimedia.org/wiki/File:1346-1353_spread_of_the_Black_Death_in_Europe_map.svg

The Holy Roman Empire lacked a powerful central figure of authority until 1312 with the uncontested election of Henry VII. He, as well as his successors, invested a great deal of effort to return power and control to the imperial crown. The German princes continued to resist and make it difficult for the emperor to regain his authority; however, that wasn't the only challenge.

During the 14th century, the bubonic plague spread to the Holy Roman Empire. The source of the 1347 outbreak was Italy, and in just three years, it had spread throughout the German territories. A third of the European population died in the infamous Black Death. The cause was long-distance trade between merchants who traveled from the Italian coasts to the Middle East and Asia. The Silk Road had been opened to the Europeans by the Mongols who ruled over China, a land that had already been suffering from the plague since the 1330s. The merchants brought the plague with them to the Italian ports, from which it spread through the many trade routes that went from the Mediterranean across the entirety of mainland Europe, Scandinavia, and even Scotland.

The plague didn't just cause a massive number of deaths. With it came a massive economic crisis that led to famine throughout the continent. As poverty increased, more and more people became malnourished and too weak to fight disease. Consequently, a radical religious sect called the Flagellants emerged in Europe as well as the Holy Roman Empire. They were famous for owning no possessions and scourging themselves while traveling from one town to the next, seeking atonement. Due to poverty and death surrounding every town, the sect grew in influence and started blaming and persecuting the Jewish communities as well as other minorities.

During those times, the Jews were permitted to live in special areas and only in certain cities where the local administration or the clergy would benefit from them. In a way, they received special protection despite the persecution due to their financial and medical expertise. But, at the same time, they were hated by the common citizens who either despised them due to their religious practices or were envious of their wealth. The Flagellant sect contributed to spreading this hatred further throughout the empire. The Jews were now blamed for poisoning the wells and spreading the disease, even though they were suffering and dying from the plague the same as Christians. The hatred and fear led to a massacre, and many Jewish communities were destroyed. However, these dreadful events were not something that occurred only in German territory. Hatred towards the Jews had already existed for at least a few centuries. For example, during the 11th century, the crusaders that marched to fight the Muslims often stopped in several locations on their route to kill Jews. In fact, in some places—Germany included—the Jews were forced to dress in such a way to be easily identified. This included the display of the Star of David on their clothing.

The Flagellants continued to preach that God was punishing humanity for its corruption, pointing fingers specifically at the Vatican and the Catholic Church. As their word spread, the common people started blaming each other, whether they were Christian or Jewish, and trust in the secular administration plummeted as well. The papacy could not remain idle and immediately marked the Flagellants as a heretical organization. However, the clergy had suffered as well, both from the plague and the economic crisis, vastly diminishing their resources and influence.

In the Holy Roman Empire, the plague and conflicts between the nobles pushed the crown to launch a series of reforms to settle the problem of succession. Previous elections were repeatedly interrupted by conflicts and various political interests. Therefore, the idea of what the empire meant had to be clarified and changed. The first reform was made in 1356 with the signing of the Golden Bull, which defined all the procedures and protocols that had to take place during the election of the emperor.

From that point on, the emperor would be elected by the seven Kurfürsten (electors). Four of them were secular electors, namely the Duke of Saxony, the King of Bohemia, the Margrave of Brandenburg, and the Count Palatine of the Rhine. The other three were the Archbishops of Cologne, Mainz, and Trier. However, while these changes did bring some measure of order, the Holy Roman Empire was still politically unstable and unpredictable. The emperor lacked the centralized power and authority he needed to keep the princes under control. Thus, they frequently fought against each other for dominance, and the common people, as well as the economy, continued to suffer the consequences. The empire continued its descent until the Habsburgs took the throne and launched a campaign of massive reforms.

The First Habsburgs and the Beginning of Imperial Reformation

Frederick III of Habsburg was the first of his dynasty to take the imperial crown of the Holy Roman Empire. However, the country was still in chaos from the futile wars between the great houses. He made little progress in imperial reform, but he paved the way for his son, Maximilian I.

Maximilian succeeded in organizing a meeting with the electors and the German princes to debate the reformation of the empire. The historical Diet of Worms was held in 1495, wherein the nobles agreed to a series of changes.

One of the greatest reforms was the establishment of the Reichskammergericht, which was essentially an imperial court of justice tasked with settling the disputes and conflicts throughout the empire. Maximilian was also successful in creating an imperial court, known as the Reichshofrat, as a balancing measure that would give the emperor some authority and influence.

Progress was being made—but slowly—as discussions, debates, and negotiations resumed between the princes and the emperor. Another important reform was the creation of a regional administration system, known as the Imperial Circles (Reichskreise). There were six administrations implemented to manage the six major regions, and they officially started working in 1512. During the same year, the empire changed its official name, declaring itself the Holy Roman Empire of the German Nation. This move, together with the reforms, could be considered evidence of the rising of a unified German identity.

But the most important reform during this time of chaos was the declaration of the "Ewiger Landfriede," which translates to "eternal peace." Attempts to accomplish such a reform had been made since the 12th century, but with minor success. The concept behind it was to ban the German nobles' rights to armed conflict against other fellow noblemen. Until the Diet of Worms, any dispute or conflict between noblemen could be settled through armed conflict. This was the main cause of economic and social chaos and the lack of a unified identity. From 1495 onward, all disputes and conflicts would have to be settled at the court through a legal process and not on the battlefield.

Emperor Maximilian didn't dictate these reforms, and he was even against some of them. However, with their implementation, the Holy Roman Empire started enjoying a newly-found peace, which gradually boosted the economy and improved the lives of citizens throughout the empire.

Chapter 5 – The Reformation

The religious revolution known as the Reformation marked the beginning of a new era in the Holy Roman Empire. While its touch wasn't felt in society and politics until the 16th century, the Reformation started emerging two centuries earlier. The 14th century had gone through a series of massive transformations and crises, the most well-known of which were the Black Death of 1347 and the Papal Schism. These events made the German people, as well as other Europeans, think about their religion, church, and society itself.

The people experienced an internal crisis and, consequently, challenged the clergy's authority and the way they interpreted the Holy Scriptures. Various personalities, such as Jan Hus from Bohemia and John Wycliffe from England, emerged to criticize the church's privileges. However, during the 14th century, they lacked the ability to spread their opinions and views far and wide and were eventually executed. Both became precursors for the Reformation.

Hus was summoned to the Council of Constance, where he was condemned for heresy. Even though he went under imperial protection, he was executed. This event led to a rebellion in Bohemia that lasted for fourteen years. The church silenced Hus and Wycliffe, but after the spiritual crisis during the days of the

Black Death, they could no longer silence the people's desire for reform. In the following century, the church authorities would become overwhelmed by the need for an inner religious experience.

Technology Paves the Way

Until the beginning of the 15th century, ideas and opinions were being spread painstakingly slowly by word of mouth and handwritten works. Pamphlets and books were written and copied entirely by hand, taking months before they were ready to be sent to other corners of the realm. This process also involved many mistakes, errors, and the occasional reinterpretation of the text. Printing did exist to some degree, but even that was entirely manual. Craftsmen had to carve the pages they wanted to copy into wooden blocks and then use them to print one page at a time by stamping. This process yielded better results than the handwritten copies; however, it was expensive, and printed works were only sent to rich monasteries, noblemen, and wealthy merchants.

All of that would change in the German city of Mainz, where Johannes Gutenberg would invent the printing press in the 1440s, an invention that played a key role in launching a revolution throughout Europe.

Gutenberg worked with metal, mainly crafting highly polished metal mirrors. But he wasn't well known before his famous invention. History took note of him in 1439 when he was sued by an investor who partnered with him to create the printing press. The court took an inventory of every item in his workshop, where various metals and printing types were noted.

As a skilled metalworker, Gutenberg first invented a special alloy by combining antimony with lead and tin. This resulted in a strong material perfect for molding durable printing types that would last a long time without deforming. Also, he invented a new oil-based ink so that his printed works could last much longer than those written in traditional ink. Finally, in the coming years, he created the first printing press model, using wine presses for inspiration for the mechanical parts. At first, printing was still expensive because his first model was still inefficient. However, he made improvements during the time he printed presumably 200 copies of the Bible, known today as the Gutenberg Bibles.

After he improved the design of the printing press, Gutenberg's revolutionary invention started spreading throughout Europe. The written word started becoming available to almost everyone. Before that, a skilled scribe could produce only a few pages per workday, and a wooden block printing press could produce a few dozen. Gutenberg's press was capable of printing more than 3,000 pages per day. But more importantly, printing became affordable, and periodical texts could be produced in mass. Before the printing press, only important works, such as religious and scholarly texts, were being copied or printed.

A few decades after the invention of the printing press, ideas started spreading like wildfire throughout the Holy Roman Empire, as well as most of Europe. With hundreds of books, religious materials, and intellectual works being produced every year, the Reformation was underway, as well as the humanist movement.

Humanism

Gutenberg's printing press is one of the main reasons the humanism movement spread throughout the German territories. Its driving goal was to find and restore many of the ancient texts from the classical age to recover the lost knowledge and wisdom. These texts were copied and widely spread, leading to a better and more diverse education in Europe. The humanists began challenging the authority of the Catholic Church and the way they interpreted the holy texts.

Initially, humanism started spreading from Italy. The movement was secular for the most part, focusing on social problems and civic values. Italian humanism was pushed and sponsored by the nobility and the wealthy merchant class. On the other hand, in the Holy Roman Empire, humanism became a movement focused on the spiritual aspect of society. In German cities, the movement was spreading from the universities, which, during those times, were attached to the church.

Furthermore, German humanism was less elitist than its Italian counterpart, and it contained a populist element. In other words, it was primarily aimed towards the masses instead of the intellectual and wealthy classes. The printing press allowed humanistic ideas to spread to the public, and new humanist schools were being raised to educate a new Christian generation. While the Italian scholars focused on the famous classical philosophers, politicians, and orators such as Cicero and Plato, the Germans preferred to study and interpret religious texts. They began researching the earliest biblical sources that were written in Hebrew, Latin, and Greek, seeking out the original Christian practices to reform the church.

One of the most famous humanists north of the Alps was Erasmus of Rotterdam, who lived from 1466 to 1536. He and other humanists were deeply embedded in the church, but they desired to reform the institution and its practices. During these pre-Reformation decades, the humanists gathered thousands of books written in the aforementioned languages to translate and study. Consequently, some of them rediscovered the philosophical and religious concept of Hermeticism.

Hermeticism dates to the first century CE, according to Plutarch. Its doctrine claims that there is one God and that he is present in every religion. The scholars sent out to scour the monasteries for ancient texts found numerous volumes discussing this religion. These sacred texts formed what is known as the Corpus Hermeticum, and they shared information about topics such as magic, alchemy, and astrology. These discoveries during the Renaissance period led the humanist scientists and scholars to explore the concept of magic. The Catholic Church did not appreciate their pursuit of cabbalistic mysticism and the occult. The church condemned their actions, even though some of the hermeticists were monastery abbots and bishops.

The rediscovery of ancient knowledge led to a desire to research the original biblical sources of the Christian faith. The humanists sought a purer translation, and they printed new versions of the Penitential Psalms and other Scriptures to spread the new teachings. These actions, led by the most revered humanist in the north, Desiderius Erasmus, would trigger the Protestant Reformation.

Erasmus of Rotterdam was a pious Christian, and despite his critique of the Catholic clergy, he did not abandon Catholicism. He was a firm believer in a personal relationship with God instead of signs and rituals. However, his writings, especially the printing of the Greek New Testament, laid the groundwork for the Reformation. He became one of the earliest celebrities in the print world, and his works that called for the reformation of the Christian way of life resonated with many scholars and common folk on the continent. But his intention wasn't to break the church apart. He was loyal to the Vatican and the papacy. His goal was to clean the clergy of corruption and bad practices. However, his main work, the Greek New Testament, fueled the beginning of the Reformation in the Holy Roman Empire and thus did damage to the Catholic Church.

Martin Luther and the Protestant Reformation

Portrait of Martin Luther
https://commons.wikimedia.org/wiki/File:Martin_Luther_by_Cranach-restoration.jpg

During the Renaissance period, the papacy did not focus entirely on religious activity and moral guidance. It was one of the most important benefactors contributing to the emergence of artists and scholars. The popes also acted as secular rulers over their domains, the Papal States. The most famous pope during those times was Alexander VI, and he wasn't widely known for his piety and Catholic resolve. His goal was to amass wealth and dominate over the Papal States with the help of his warlord son, Cesare Borgia, who was depicted as a ruthless character in Niccolò Machiavelli's famous work titled *The Prince*. Pope Julius II is another such example: he was known as the warrior pope for waging several wars during his papal appointment. These Renaissance popes may have been important patrons of the artists that sparked a cultural revolution, but their focus on power sunk the Catholic Church in scandal.

The clergy's corruption continued to deepen while the people were seeking an honest spiritual experience and religious guidance. The anti-papal sentiment reached its height when the church started selling indulgences. These certificates were either bought or received as a reward, relieving the bearer of any guilt, sin, and punishment. The clergy went as far as specifying the amount of time that would be spent in purgatory for certain sins and reducing that time by selling an indulgence. This became a popular scheme that brought the clergy ample revenue. The masses were quite content for a while. On the other hand, Christian scholars and humanists like Erasmus condemned the practice and mocked the greed and decadence of bishops and priests.

But not all clerics and priests agreed with the indulgence practice. Martin Luther was one of them. He was a priest and theology professor who would soon become the main figure of the German Reformation. He and other humanists watched the situation develop with great concern until it reached its high point in 1515. Two years before that, Pope Leo X ascended to the papal seat. He belonged to the famous and powerful Medici family from

Florence, and he wanted to be seen and remembered differently from all the popes who came before him.

Pope Leo X was an important patron of the arts, investing enormous amounts of wealth in talented artists, humanist scholars, and especially into the project to rebuild Saint Peter's Basilica. However, the papacy's treasure wasn't bottomless, and he needed a new source of wealth. In 1515, Pope Leo declared a new type of indulgence that could be sold by the clergy: the plenary indulgence. By purchasing this document from the church, a relative would be able to release the soul of a loved one from purgatory. This type of indulgence was also being sold in the Holy Roman Empire under the authority of the Archbishop of Mainz and Magdeburg because he needed funds to settle the large debt he'd amassed to win his election. Half of the profits made by selling the plenary indulgences in the territory he administered would go into his own pockets.

Martin Luther, who was a professor of theology at the University of Wittenberg, became increasingly concerned with this practice. He was also outraged when he learned that the archbishop was convincing the buyers that the certificate would instantly free them of all sins and any requirements of penance and confession. In 1517, Luther was so worried about innocent Christians following a path to damnation that he wrote a letter to the archbishop, officially noting his objections against this practice. But his warning was ignored, so Luther started writing a set of theological theses on the subject (this was a common way to stir up debate within the church).

Luther's collection is known as the Ninety-five Theses, and they were sent to the archbishop and posted on the walls of the university. He challenged the indulgence sellers to a debate, but he did not go directly against the indulgences themselves. Luther was careful because it was the pope who allowed these certificates to be sold, and he couldn't go against him at the time. He disputed the corrupt sales method only in the German territories.

However, despite Luther's caution, the printing press spread the word about his attack on the church. His theses were meant for internal debate between theologians and scholars, but the press made his works available in every tavern and workshop in the Holy Roman Empire and beyond. Martin Luther quickly went from a simple priest and professor to one of the most famous people in all the lands of Germany. His theses were being discussed even in Rome.

The pope decided to silence Luther through internal authority by asking the order of Augustinian monks to which Luther belonged to show him the errors of his ways. However, during the order's convocation, Luther presented his case in such an impressive manner that he drew the other monks to his side. Consequently, the Dominican order went against the Augustinians to silence Luther. They were famous inquisitors who already had a rivalry with the Augustinian order, so they readily defended the archbishop.

Since the matter wasn't resolved, the pope demanded Luther's presence in Rome within two months. Luther knew that this meant excommunication or perhaps even execution. The same thing happened to predecessors like Jan Hus. So, he sought the protection of Frederick of Saxony, the patron of Wittenberg University. Frederick, an elector, immediately sided with Luther as the famous professor who had placed his university on the European map and could be used for other ambitions against the papacy and the emperor.

Pope Leo couldn't act severely because his authority in the Holy Roman Empire wasn't as solid as before. The German citizens and nobles were gradually pulling away from the Catholic Church, complaining that too much money went to Rome and the papacy wasn't investing nearly enough. Nationalist sentiment was spreading. Furthermore, the election for the new emperor was approaching, and the pope hoped to push his candidate on the throne because he was worried about the Habsburgs taking over. He needed the German princes and electors, including Frederick, to be on his side so that they could cast a favorable vote.

Luther continued publishing new works that fueled the debate against Catholic clergy and the sale of indulgences. In the following years, he grew in popularity: historians estimate that over 10,000 of his pamphlets were printed throughout the Holy Roman Empire, both in German and Latin. These works marked the beginning of the Protestant Reformation. In 1520, Pope Leo issued a decree demanding Luther to retract more than forty of his works due to certain errors that didn't fit with the church's views. Luther refused and burned the decree the day he gathered a congregation at the university. This act declared that the pope no longer had authority. As a reply, Pope Leo issued a new decree the following year in which he excommunicated Luther and ordered the clergy to find and destroy his works. Luther's followers gathered in his defense, making it clear to everyone that the Germans were breaking away from the Catholic Church.

In 1521, Luther's presence was demanded at the Diet of Worms, where the new Holy Roman Emperor Charles V, the ruler of Spain and a Habsburg, convened with the nobles. The new emperor was powerful and feared due to the vastness of wealth and power he had gathered thanks to the lucrative Spanish colonies. Even the German noble houses feared him because he had enough power to make them submit to a central authority: himself. Furthermore, Charles was a pious Catholic, which made the Protestants anxious. But Luther was under Frederick of Saxony's protection, so he traveled to Worms. The emperor was determined to bring order to his lands, so he condemned Luther and his works. Charles didn't arrest him, but Luther did become an outlaw. However, this act didn't stop the Protestant Reformation.

Frederick arranged to have Luther taken to the Wartburg Castle, where he would be protected to continue his work. From there, Luther began translating the original Scriptures to build a German Bible. He succeeded in creating the German New Testament by seeking inspiration from Erasmus' work, the Greek New Testament. The new Bible went to print in 1530, and it's estimated that, by 1546 (the year of Luther's death), over half a million copies were printed. Furthermore, the publishing of the German Bible had a secondary but equally important effect. It served to standardize the German language throughout the German lands. Up to that point, there were many different dialects throughout the empire.

The emperor couldn't do anything against Luther despite the edict he issued at Worms. The German people supported the Protestant Reformation, and Luther was being protected by a few German princes, such as Frederick of Saxony. However, Charles banned Luther's works in the lands over which he had direct control and even executed several Protestants that he judged as heretics. The Reformation was about to become violent.

In the following years, several followers of Lutheran teaching began spreading their new ideas throughout the German territories. Their preaching against the church, the emperor, and feudalism sparked a series of revolts among the imperial knights and clergy, as well as the peasantry. The rebellions were violent. At first, Luther supported them, feeling their anguish, but he tried to resolve everything peacefully by mediating between the church and the rebels. However, he was unsuccessful, and the violence continued. Luther feared that these rebellions were endangering his theological revolution, so he printed a new work in which he sided with the imperial authorities and supported violent action against the rising peasantry. Consequently, both Protestant and Catholic German noblemen raised arms against the rebels and vanquished them. It is estimated that the professional military killed more than 100,000 peasants, together with their leaders, some of whom were Luther's close students and followers, such as Thomas Muntzer.

In 1525, the Protestant peasants' rebellion officially ended, but the Reformation continued with what we now call the Princes' Reformation. Backed by the Saxon prince, Luther started building the new Lutheran Church that would confiscate the properties of the Catholic Church and replace all their rituals. In the following years, the wealth that was taken from the German Catholics was enough to fund the state-supported Lutheran administration. Luther also directly contributed to a new manual that would guide the Protestant pastors on their responsibilities and religious duties.

While Luther was leading the Protestant Reformation in Saxony, he wasn't the only reformer. In Switzerland, Huldrych Zwingli was leading his own reformation beginning in 1522. His view of Protestantism was more liberal than Luther's, and they didn't agree on multiple points. This posed a problem to Luther's dream of a Protestant Germany because Zwingli's reformation quickly started spreading to the southern German cities. The Reformation was in danger because, if divided, the Catholic Church could easily go against each group separately. Seeking common ground, the two reformers met in 1529 to discuss the issue. However, the meeting failed because Luther and Zwingli could not agree on all points, and no compromise was made.

Despite the divide, the German princes continued supporting the Saxon model of Protestantism under Luther. The emperor's edict was ignored for the most part, but Charles grew increasingly worried about having two different religious views and institutions in his empire. Furthermore, he feared that he might lose support from the princes who were converting from Catholicism. In 1526, he allowed the German nobles to decide how to deal with the Protestant movement in their states. However, in 1529, he reversed his decision, going against the Protestant Reformation once more and, in 1531, demanded them to restore the Catholic Church's properties.

Fearing the wrath of the emperor and the Catholic Church, the Protestant princes began forging mutual defense alliances with each other and their neighbors. The divide between the two religions was creating a rift in German society, and it was becoming wider with each passing year. In the hope of healing this rift, the Diet of Regensburg was organized in 1541. Theology experts from both sides met to discuss the issues and seek a compromise. The meeting was another disaster, and it greatly angered Charles. The emperor launched a campaign of negotiation with the French, as well as the Turks—who, until then, had been his most hated enemies. His goal was to war against the Protestants, and so he did.

With Luther's death in 1546, the emperor marched against the Protestant princes and defeated them. Two years later, he issued a new decree declaring the restoration of the Catholic faith throughout the empire. However, Charles was betrayed by the prince of Saxony, Maurice, who allied with the French dynasty of Valois. The Valois were the enemies of the Habsburg dynasty, and with their help and support from the remaining Protestant princes, a new war commenced between the two sides. In 1552, the Princes' War wreaked havoc on the emperor's military. Charles lost in this conflict and was forced to later abdicate in 1555. The emperor accepted his defeat, retiring to a Spanish monastery, and peace was declared at Augsburg.

After decades of conflict in the name of the Reformation, the princes were given the right to choose between Catholicism and Protestantism in the lands or cities they governed. The people were obligated to respect their decision and to follow the faith of their prince. Any other religion was forbidden, including Zwingli's version of the Protestant Reformation. Peace between the two sides would hold over the next six decades until the rise of a new wave of Catholicism and a new form of Protestantism known as Calvinism.

Chapter 6 – The Thirty Years' War

When Charles V abdicated, he recognized that the empire was too great to be managed by one Habsburg emperor, so he divided the territories. The eastern corner of the empire, mainly Austria and Bohemia, was given to the Austrian branch of his family, who we refer to as the Austrian Habsburgs. This family would dominate that area for the next three centuries. As for the Holy Roman Empire, Charles pushed for his brother Ferdinand I to be elected, and so he was in 1558.

The situation was complicated, as the Protestant princes had started to officially solidify their position. But Ferdinand, just like his brother, was a pious Catholic. He supported the diminishing power of the Catholic Church and invested in its reformation. While the Catholic Reformation began at the same time as the Protestant Reformation under the influence of Catholic humanists like Erasmus, it didn't become drastic until 1545, when the Council of Trent was held. In the following two decades, the pope met there on occasion with the high clergy to discuss the corruption and decisions that affected the religious life of the German people. Among his goals was to end the schism that was happening and refute Luther's teaching. But by labeling the Protestants as heretics and forcing the church to become more rigid and inflexible, the Council of Trent had the opposite effect: the rift between the two faiths widened. However, the pope managed to slow down the spread of Lutheranism and even stopped it completely in some parts of Europe.

Calvinism Emerges

Jean Calvin

While Luther's Protestant wave was slowing down, Calvinism started spreading and reinforcing the movement. Named after Jean (John) Calvin, a French Protestant reformer accused of heresy, Calvinism took hold in Geneva between the 1530s and 1540s. Calvin fled to the Swiss city to avoid the French authorities and shaped it into his vision of a Protestant theocracy. The main difference between Calvinism and Lutheranism at the time was the fact that Calvin focused more on conservative ideals and discipline, and his main goal was to spread his theology everywhere on the European continent.

Protestants flocked to Geneva, craving a so-called heavenly city in the middle of a corrupt world full of sin. Scholars, merchants, and crafters moved to the city, thus sparking an economic boom. The Swiss city became a beacon of Protestantism that allowed Calvin to print his theological works and spread them throughout Europe with the help of his missionaries.

Calvin's missionaries risked their lives to spread his teachings, especially in France and the Holy Roman Empire. In France, Protestantism was entirely forbidden, but in the empire, it depended on each prince (per the Augsburg peace treaty, the princes could determine the faith that would be followed throughout their territories). Calvinism and Protestantism, in general, were particularly successful with nobles who desired a decentralized authority.

The first German prince to adopt the new faith was Frederick the Pious, the elector of the Rhineland-Palatinate. Initially, he was a Lutheran, but he gradually moved on to Calvinism by allowing Calvin's missionaries to teach at Heidelberg University and to take positions within the Palatine Church. From Heidelberg, Calvinism would gradually spread throughout the empire, although Louis VI, Frederick's successor, tried to restore the Lutheran faith.

Catholicism was undergoing its own reformation, and it was strengthening while Calvinism continued to spread. The two faiths were causing tension among the Germans, and they were about to clash. The rise of Calvinism played a significant role in causing the destruction and chaos of the Thirty Years' War, during which religious conflict led to violence, but it cannot be solely blamed. During the same period, the European noble houses were competing against each other. Eventually, the Spanish and Austrian Habsburgs confronted their French, Danish, and Swedish adversaries. Ultimately, the war was ignited from both political and religious pressure.

Conflicts began erupting as soon as the early 1600s. In 1607, Maximilian I of Bavaria invaded and took control of Donauworth. The city was occupied to defend the Catholic population, which was the minority. The duke acted with the support of the emperor and began the process of restoring the Catholic faith.

As a response to Maximilian's actions, in 1608, the Protestant princes forged an alliance that became known as the Protestant Union, under the command of Frederick IV, Elector Palatine. But in the Holy Roman Empire, the Catholic Church still enjoyed a great deal of support, so they formed their own military alliance called the Catholic League just one year later, with Maximilian as its chief representative and commander. Maximilian represented the Catholic faith and Frederick the Protestant faith, even though they were related—both were part of the Wittelsbach dynasty. The two sides were originally supposed to be alliances to guarantee security and good diplomatic relationships. However, it didn't take long for both sides to turn into little more than military factions eager to go to war against each other.

The Thirty Years' War Begins

The year 1618 marks the beginning of the Thirty Years' War, and it all started with an uprising in Bohemia. The people rebelled when Ferdinand II of the Habsburg dynasty began enforcing the Catholic faith in Bohemia. Prague, then the capital of Bohemia and the city of reformer Jan Hus, did not support the emperor and was against the Catholic reformation. The city was dominated by Calvinists. However, in 1617, Ferdinand II became the king of Bohemia, and one of his goals was to restore Catholicism. His first act was to reorganize the Catholic mass at the same church where Jan Hus preached. This action angered the Protestants, and in 1618 they rose and apprehended the three royal representatives of the Habsburg Crown, throwing them out the window of the government palace in Prague. This revolt is now known as the "Defenestration of Prague." However, the royal officials survived the fall.

In 1619, Ferdinand II officially became the Holy Roman Emperor, and the conflict escalated. Protestant nobles in Prague issued a proclamation that declared Bohemia an elective monarchy. They disposed of Ferdinand and chose a new king. Frederick V, a Calvinist who ruled the Rhineland-Palatinate and was also the leader of the Protestant League, was the perfect candidate, and he ruled as king of Bohemia for one year. Because of the shortness of his rule, he remains known to history as the "winter king." Ferdinand was angered by the coronation of Frederick. He was elected Holy Roman Empire only three months earlier, and he viewed the coronation of a Protestant as a direct attack on his imperial rule. To challenge Frederick, he needed to raise an army, and nearby Bavaria offered the perfect ground to do so. Bavaria was under the rule of Duke Maximilian I, Ferdinand's ally. As it bordered Bohemia, it was a natural choice from which to launch an invasion. At the Battle of White Mountain on November 8, 1620, imperial forces crushed the army of King Frederick, as none of his Protestant allies showed up. Frederick was exiled to Holland, and his rule in Bohemia ended.

Ferdinand took over the Palatinate and reestablished his authority in Bohemia. Catholicism was restored by force, and many Bohemians were punished for being Protestants. Consequently, thousands of Protestants abandoned their homeland and emigrated to different parts of the empire. Ferdinand appointed a governor of Bohemia, through which he could control the kingdom and extract revenues. Czech nobleman Albrecht von Wallenstein was the first governor and military leader. As soon as he came to the position, he started gathering a mercenary army that would serve the imperial needs. This army had the first chance to show its might in 1525, when the Danish king, Christian IV (1577-1648), invaded Germany. He was a Lutheran, so one of the reasons for the invasion was religion— but it wasn't the only one. He also had an interest in the Baltic region and hoped he could claim the territories of northern Germany for Denmark. But the army of the Danish king was no match for the imperial army under the two brilliant commanders, Johann Tserclaes, Count of Tilly, and Albrecht von Wallenstein, governor of Bohemia. The two Catholic commanders easily beat Christian IV in a series of battles. The Danish were forced back to Denmark, and Ferdinand was now unopposed in his rule.

The height of Ferdinand's power came when the emperor issued the Edict of Restitution in March 1629. With the edict, he demanded all the Catholic lands confiscated by Protestants since the Peace of Augsburg (1555) to be returned to Catholic rulers. The Augsburg settlement had a clause named "Ecclesiastical Reservation," which guaranteed that no further Catholic lands were to be conquered by the Protestants. However, this clause was not enforced for eighty years, and Ferdinand sought to retroactively enforce it with the use of the imperial army. Furthermore, Ferdinand's edict sought to forcefully re-Catholicize not only the territories but also the people.

In 1630, Ferdinand dismissed Wallenstein. The military commander was unpopular with both Protestants and Catholics, who put pressure on their emperor. Since Ferdinand needed supporters for the election of his son, Ferdinand III, as king of Romans, he complied with the people. But this decision proved to be very costly, as in July of the same year, Germany was invaded by Swedish King Gustavus Adolphus Vasa, simply known as Gustav II (1594–1632). He was a very pious Lutheran, and he came to help fellow Protestants against the Edict of Restitution. As with the Danish king, he had an interest in the Baltics, which he had already taken from the Poles through wars (1626–1629). Gustav II had the full support of the Protestant rulers of Germany, and in 1631, the imperial and Swedish armies clashed in the Battle of Breitenfeld. Gustav II was a great and innovative tactician, and he deployed more nimble, linear formations of his army. The imperial force, commanded by the Count of Tilly, still used the old Spanish formation, which was slow to move but hard to break. But the Swedish king had no trouble crushing his enemies' lines with the innovative use of firepower and mobility. By March 1632, he invaded Bavaria, having crushed the count on the battlefield. At another battle, near Rain on the River Lech, Gustav II crushed the Catholic League with skillful usage of artillery and cavalry. The Count of Tilly died in this battle, and his troops, having no commander, scattered across the battlefield in panic. Bavaria was conquered by the Swedes, and from it, they launched attacks on the Habsburg heartland—Austria.

In May of 1632, when Gustav II entered Munich (the capital of Bavaria), Ferdinand II was forced to recall Albrecht von Wallenstein as fear from the Protestants rose. The brilliant military leader was quick to organize a new imperial army and, with it, successfully confronted the Swedes. In November of 1632, Wallenstein met Gustav II at the Battle of Lützen. The imperial force didn't fare well at the beginning of the conflict, but Swedish King Gustav II was shot during the battle as he led the cavalry charge. Swedes did not abandon their mission in Germany when their king died, but fortune turned her back to the Protestants. Without their charismatic and brilliant leader, they couldn't keep up with the Catholics. The conflict came to a stalemate for the next two years.

In 1634, Ferdinand II realized Wallenstein was too ambitious, so he plotted to get rid of him. Soon, he employed several lieutenants of the imperial army to assassinate the general. The leader of the imperial forces was murdered in his bed in Eger, but Ferdinand II won his greatest victory at this time, proving he didn't need Wallenstein to end the war. In September 1634, at the Battle of Nördlingen, the imperial army was joined with the Spanish infantry, and together, they managed to crush the Saxon-Swedish alliance. This battle ended Swedish dominance in Germany, and the Protestants suffered their greatest defeat of the Thirty Years' War.

The German Protestants were forced to seek a separate peace with Ferdinand, which was signed in 1635 under the name Peace of Prague. The emperor granted a major concession to the Protestants to secure peace within the empire. Unfortunately, the hostilities didn't end because the foreign rulers involved would not let the German Protestants enjoy their peace.

The Spanish warred with the Dutch, and even though they were involved with their German cousins in the Thirty Years' War, the Peace of Prague didn't concern them. The Swedes weren't involved in the peace, either, and they continued their fight against the imperial forces. The French, the longtime enemies of the Habsburgs, supplied the Swedes for the war with the Holy Roman Empire, as it was against their interests to allow Ferdinand to consolidate his position as an emperor. French statesman and ardent Catholic Cardinal Richelieu allied with Protestant Swedes and the Dutch. To keep the war with the empire certain, he also started a conflict with the Spanish and Austrian Habsburgs. Europe entered the final and most devastating stage of the Thirty Years' War.

The last decade of the conflict brought agony to the empire's civilians. The battles themselves were few and far apart, but the mercenary armies employed by both sides were ravaging the countryside to destroy the provisions for their enemies. Besides destroying fertile land and cattle, the armies enjoyed torturing the civilians, raping the women, and burning the homes of common people. Thousands of starving villagers were forced to abandon their land and seek fortune in another area, leaving whole German territories completely depopulated. Aside from poverty and hunger, peasants were hit hard by diseases, and tens of thousands of them died in agony. Today, the estimation is that, at the end of the Thirty Years' War, Germany lost at least one third of its population. Aside from the war, Germany was engulfed in the great European witch hunt, which only added to depopulation. There was no central authority to overlook the trials in which thousands of suspected witches lost their lives. Territorial princes and magistrates were free to punish the women accused of witchery as they saw fit, and most sentenced them to death. Confessions were forced out of the frightened and powerless women, and torture was considered a valid means of extorting a confession.

The war, which had strictly taken place within the borders of the Holy Roman Empire, finally spilled out, taking over much of the continent. Conflicts occurred in the Netherlands, Bohemia, Denmark, and Italy. France sent its troops to Germany, but they fared very poorly, and the Spanish forces easily pushed them back to France. Having financed both Sweden and their army, the French realized that their involvement was proving too costly. The successor of Cardinal Richelieu, Cardinal Mazarin, was eager to end the conflict. In fact, by 1643, all major forces involved in the war wanted to end it. Peace negotiations started in the Westphalian cities of Osnabrück and Münster, but that doesn't mean the war ended. The conflict continued parallel to the peace talks. By 1645, Ferdinand III, the successor of the Holy Roman Emperor Ferdinand II, suffered a series of defeats that forced him to seek peace. In 1648, the Peace of Westphalia was finally concluded. More than 150 delegates signed the treaty as the representatives of the Holy Roman Emperor and the rulers of Spain, France, Netherlands, and German principalities. The thirty years of warfare finally ended, and a new political order was brought to the empire.

With the Peace of Westphalia, Sweden got an important part of the Baltic territories, but it was France that profited the most. The emperor was willing to grant most of Alsace and Lorraine to the French. The Dutch won the recognition of their independence by Spain, and the Rhine Palatinate was given to the Calvinist Wittelsbach line of Frederick V. In Germany, territories were restored to the provisions established in 1555 by the Peace of Augsburg. However, the rulers of German territories were now free to choose the religion of their domain, and even then, the people could practice whichever religion they chose. The Peace of

Westphalia fundamentally changed the political scene within the empire. The emperor's authority was significantly diminished, as the 300 princes of the empire had formal sovereignty over their territories. They were also allowed to conduct foreign policies without imperial restrictions. By allowing this to happen, Ferdinand III forever ended the Habsburg dream of converting the Holy Roman Empire into a centralized empire, such as Sweden or France.

Chapter 7 – The Age of Enlightenment

In 17th and 18th-century Europe, it was uncommon for a kingdom to be ruled by a female. But the Austrian Hamburg Emperor Charles VI (1685-1740) had no sons, and he had to ensure that his eldest daughter, Maria Theresa, inherited his throne. He not only issued an edict that legitimized female succession in Austria but also actively worked on persuading the other European rulers to accept Maria Theresa as his heir. Charles' Pragmatic Sanction, a decree which ensured Maria's succession, was accepted by almost all neighboring kingdoms. However, some rulers hoped they could profit from the dynastic instability in Habsburg Austria and declined to accept the Pragmatic Sanction. One of these was the ambitious king of Prussia, Friedrich Wilhelm I (r.1713-1740).

Maria Theresa (1717-1780) was only twenty-three years old when her father died in 1740, leaving her the throne of Austria. But when she tried to establish herself as the empress, she was denied this privilege by the Prussian ruler who contested her claim to the throne. He invaded Austria in December of the same year and occupied Silesia, a strategically important part of Austria. Inspired by the Prussian defection, other rulers who had previously accepted

Pragmatic Sanction now declined the young empress her crown. Among them were France, Spain, Saxony, and Bavaria. Facing such mighty enemies, Maria had few options. However, Hungary accepted her and crowned her their queen, which allowed her to use the Hungarian army as a defense against her attackers. Austria was already invaded by the Bavarians who occupied Vienna and by the French who entered Bohemia when Maria Theresa personally traveled to Hungary to appeal to the nobles. Their queen had just given birth to her first son, and holding the newborn tightly in her arms, she addressed the Hungarians. Her famous appeal and her persona of a queen mother in danger were enough to buy her the loyalty of the Hungarian nobles. Soon, the army was marching in defense of Austria.

Eight years of succession war followed, but Maria managed to secure the crown of an empress. She lost Silesia to Prussia, but the Austrian throne was hers. Salic law still denied her the right to bear imperial titles, but she found a loophole and crowned her husband, Francis I, instead. Thus, Maria Theresa became the de facto empress of the Holy Roman Empire and, ultimately, one of the greatest rulers of the Habsburg dynasty.

Prussia

But the question must be asked: how did Prussia, a principality (duchy) that fared poorly during the Thirty Years' War, rise to power with which it could veto the emperor's decree? Prussia had ambitious rulers, the Hohenzollern dynasty, which used the period of war to gain power. The lands owned by Hohenzollern were small and scattered all over northern Germany. However, the family united and formed Brandenburg-Prussia, which included Pomerania. The territories were known under the common name Prussia, but Brandenburg belonged to the Holy Roman Empire while Prussia was outside its borders. During the conflict with the Swedes in the 17th century, the leader of the Hohenzollern dynasty, Georg Wilhelm (r.1619–1640), had to flee his own country and seek refuge in Konigsberg, today's Kaliningrad (a Russian city and province on the Baltic Sea between Poland and Lithuania). It was George's successor, Friedrich Wilhelm (r.1640-1688), who reorganized the Prussian army and transformed it from a feeble military power to a juggernaut.

Friedrich's military reformation helped him change the political image of his duchy, too. Prussia was under the fiefdom of Polish rulers, but Friedrich helped the king of Poland to fend off the Swedes during the Second Northern War (1655-1660), and as a reward, Prussia was released from its feudal obligations to the Polish Crown. As the sovereign of Prussia, Friedrich ruled as an absolutist, holding all the political power in his own hands. His title was the Great Elector, and he continued to militarize the state. After all, a powerful army already helped him realize some of his ambitions, and it was key to further political influence on Europe. His son, Friedrich III (1657-1713), continued the success of Prussia by building upon his father's ambitions. In January of 1701, he crowned himself King of Prussia. The duchy became a kingdom, while he assumed the name Friedrich I of Prussia. Because Brandenburg was still within the borders of the Holy Roman Empire, Friedrich I convinced Emperor Leopold I to elevate him to the position of a king in exchange for military help against the French during the War of the Spanish Succession (1701-1714). By agreeing to elevate the ambitious Prussian duke to a royal title, Emperor Leopold I admitted his decline in power.

Prussian rulers continued to rely on military power, and the successor of Friedrich I, Friedrich Wilhelm I, was known as the "Soldier King." He converted the Prussian army into one of the most feared in Europe. However, Friedrich Wilhelm I invested in education and farming, too, raising Prussia above all other German principalities. His father made military service mandatory for the middle class, but Wilhelm decided to allow people to pay a tax if they chose not to serve. He used this money to open new schools and hospitals and to buy and store grain, which he later sold to other principalities for a much higher price. Unlike his father,

Wilhelm I never treated the royal treasury as his personal funds. Instead, he lived modestly and sold all his father's crown jewels, leaving the treasury filled with money. Wilhelm I also never started a war, even though he managed to expand his kingdom greatly. He joined the Great Northern War (1700–1721) on the side of Russia and managed to gain some of the territories in Sweden. In the east, he moved the borders of Prussia to the Memel River and invited Protestants from all over Germany to come and settle there. The rest of Germany was Catholic, and Protestants were never welcomed there, but Prussia was a Protestant state that over 20,000 people agreed to inhabit.

Friedrich Wilhelm I was succeeded by his son, Friedrich II, also known as Friedrich the Great (1712–1786). Unlike his father, Friedrich II was a philosopher and a lover of arts. Nevertheless, he proved to be a worthy successor to the Prussian throne. Only a year after his coronation, Friedrich II moved his army to Silesia, a possession of Habsburg Austria. There, he campaigned in three different wars between 1740 and 1763, in which he triumphed and took Silesia from the combined forces of Austria, France, and Russia. In 1748, Austria moved against Prussia with the hopes of gaining its territory back. While Prussia had the support of Britain only, Austria allied with France, Spain, Russia, and Saxony. The king of Prussia displayed his military genius by launching a preemptive strike on Saxony in 1756. The Austrians and their allies were confused and allowed Prussia to dominate the early years of the war. The military power of Prussia reached its full potential, and Friedrich II beat the Austrians and French in two different battles during 1757 and then the Russians a year later. Scared by the military might of its neighbors, Sweden joined the war at this point. Sweden joined Austria, and Prussia began losing territories. The Russians took its eastern parts, together with Berlin, the capital of the kingdom. However, Britain defeated France in the battles led in their overseas colonies, and this changed the course of the war in Europe. Luck seemed to be on the Prussian side as Russian

Empress Elizabeth died in 1762, leaving her empire to the incompetent Peter III (1728-1762), who pulled Russia out of the conflict. Sweden followed, and soon, Austria was alone. The Battle of Burkersdorf—the decisive battle between Prussia and Austria—occurred on July 21, 1762. Prussia won and negotiated the prewar boundaries of its kingdom, including the conquered Silesia. With the conclusion of the Seven Years War, Prussia emerged as one of the greatest powers in Europe, capable of humiliating even the great Austria.

In the following two decades, Prussia allied itself with Russia and Austria and took part in the partitioning of Poland. The province of Royal Prussia, which was a fiefdom of the Polish monarchy, was annexed during the first partitioning and renamed West Prussia. This linked East Prussia (which was part of the Holy Roman Empire) and Pomerania, and the territories ruled by Hohenzollerns were not scattered anymore. Finally, for the first time in history, they were contiguous. Two more partitionings of Poland followed, and Prussia took part in those, too—this time under the rule of Friedrich Wilhelm II (1744-1797), nephew of Friedrich II, who died without a son to succeed him. During the second partitioning of Poland, the whole western part of this monarchy was annexed by Prussia, while in the third, Prussia gained Polish territories south of East Prussia. This area was rearranged by Friedrich Wilhelm II and divided into the provinces of New Silesia, New East Prussia, and South Prussia.

Die Aufklärung (Enlightenment)

Prussia wasn't the only principality that tried to place itself on the political scene together with the greatest European powers. However, other German provinces were less successful. They realized the Holy Roman Empire's grasp on them was weakening, and the territory of Germany had suddenly become divided into hundreds of little kingdoms. However, only Prussia and Austria became relevant enough to play the game of power struggle, while the rest of the provinces were either swallowed by the bigger players or existed in irrelevancy. Foreign powers took advantage of the situation in Germany and tried to occupy some of its territories. Louis XIV of France gained Alsace between 1678 and 1681, while some smaller kingdoms tried to assert their influence through art and culture. Saxony and Bavaria became the lead examples of richness with their newly-built castles in Dresden and Munich (their respective capitals). But no matter how efficient their bureaucracy or how much personal wealth their rulers gained, the political scene of the 18th century was dominated by two European powers: Austria and Prussia, the Hohenzollerns and the Habsburgs. Their rivalry would mark the event for the next century.

But something else happened amid Prussia's efforts to dominate the European political scene. The cultural and intellectual life of Germany was going through a change. Influenced by the Enlightenment of France and Britain, the social reforms grasped by the principalities were known as the German Enlightenment, or Aufklärung. In Germany, the Enlightenment started with two great intellectuals of the 17th and 18th centuries, Christian Thomasius (1655-1728) and Gottfried Wilhelm von Leibniz (1646-1716). Christian was a professor of law at Leipzig University and, throughout his academic years, he insisted on the idea that human reason was capable of moving society to new heights. Using his principles, he ended the persecution of witches in Germany by using the rational mind to expose witchcraft as a product of human fantasy. Gottfried, on the other hand, was a philosopher and mathematician who left his mark on German science. Together with Newton, he is credited for the invention of infinitesimal calculus (known today as calculus).

The Aufklärung continued in the 18th century and brought forth great intellectuals such as Moses Mendelssohn and Immanuel Kant. They were both philosophers who worked at the same time, playing with similar ideas. In 1763, the two even competed against each other for the Berlin Prize, a literary competition. Mendelssohn won with his essay "On Evidence in the Metaphysical Sciences" and earned the status of a "protected Jew" within Prussia. Immanuel Kant came in second with his work "Inquiry Concerning the Distinctness of the Principles of Natural Theology and Morality," but he was already a renowned philosopher with many praised publications behind him. Today, Mendelssohn remains popular because of his then-controversial ideas of religious tolerance. When he was challenged by the Swiss theologian Johann Kaspar Lavater to either dispute Christian morals or convert to Christianity, he simply replied that it is possible to admire someone's morality without converting to his faith. He admitted to his friends that he admired Jesus as a historical person and believed that his moral teachings were in place. The great German philosophers supported Mendelssohn, but the controversy itself and the publicity it received took a toll on his health. Nevertheless, he started using his influence to help the position of Jews in Germany who were suffering singular, religion-based restrictions and taxes.

Immanuel Kant was probably the most influential mind of the German Enlightenment. His work, *The Critique of Pure Reason,* remains one of the most influential works of philosophy. It challenges the traditional perception of knowledge and investigates the limits of human reason itself. He claimed that both experience and reason are essential for gaining valid and objective knowledge. The German philosophers of the day admired Kant and continued to work on his ideas, but it is our modern perception of his philosophy that best illustrates his greatness. Immanuel Kant is still teaching us valuable lessons, even today.

The Aufklärung in Germany would never occur if the bourgeoisie of the empire had not grown in power. They were the educated class of society, the civil servants, the businessmen, and the jurists, and they prepared the rest of society for acceptance of the new, revolutionary ideas of philosophers such as Kant or Thomasius. During the 18th century, the middle class began to rise in power and wealth and started asserting its own influence on society. But society wasn't their only target. They also demanded the reform of the empire's institutions that were outdated and obsolete. In the end, it was this enlightened middle class that pressured their leaders to start social reform. Subsequently, enlightened absolutism (or despotism) emerged in Germany.

Responding to the public demands, German rulers started reforms and, with them, changed the nature of politics in the Holy Roman Empire. Under the influence of the Aufklärung, rulers started granting religious freedoms and religious tolerance, as well as freedom of the press and freedom of speech. Enlightened leaders of central Europe started supporting philosophers and artists through patronage, and they would offer a place at their courts to the enlightened thinkers of the 18th century. No matter how enlightened these rulers became, they were still despots who ruled with the iron fist of autocrats. Because they strongly believed in their divine right to rule over the masses, they refused to grant constitutions to their subjects. A constitution would mean the end of the absolutistic power of German princes, and they wouldn't allow it to happen. The monarchs of Germany saw themselves as divine tools placed in their positions so they could improve the lives of their subjects. Thus, they were (and are) called the enlightened absolutists. All their efforts to improve society met resentment from both nobility and commoners. The reforms proposed by the Austrian monarchs, for example, contained an absolutist nature and lacked an understanding of the traditions and customs of society.

The most well-known enlightened absolutist is king Friedrich the Great of Prussia. In his youth, he practiced the arts and was absorbed in the Aufklärung movement. He used his knowledge of the movement during his rule to reform education, making it a state-sponsored institution. He banned torture as a practice of justice and implemented religious tolerance throughout his kingdom. He was also a patron of famous French philosopher Voltaire, as well as many other writers and artists. Nevertheless, his rule was completely autocratic and marked by strict militarism. Society had the image of an ideal enlightened ruler in their minds, but Friedrich the Great was very far from it. Rulers who came somewhat closer to those ideals were Austrian monarchs Maria Theresa (1717–1780) and her eldest son Joseph II (1741–1790).

Maria Theresa successfully defended her right to be crowned queen of the Austrians and Hungarians, but as a woman, she couldn't take the title of Empress of the Holy Roman Empire. Nevertheless, she fought for the title and granted it to her husband, becoming the power behind the throne. Modern history is certain it was Maria Theresa who was the true ruler. As a de facto empress, she brought forth a variety of enlightened social reforms in areas that included education, the economy, agriculture, and the military. Once her husband died in 1765, her power didn't diminish. She continued ruling as a Dowager Empress behind her son, Holy Roman Emperor Joseph II. Through her influence, Joseph II became one of the most enlightened rulers of Europe. He modernized the administration of the Habsburg lands, extended religious tolerance throughout the empire, reduced the influence of the church on the state, and promoted free trade and free thinking. Although enlightened, Maria Theresa was more conservative than her son, and her opposition stopped Joseph from implementing all the social reforms he intended. However, when she died in 1780, the emperor was free to implement his program. In fact, he was so eager to change the world around him that he issued thousands of new edicts. But with all those edicts, he proved his autocratic grasp over the empire. He reformed the legal system and the financial system of the empire, abolished serfdom, and secularized some of the church's numerous properties. He also established compulsory elementary education for all citizens, abolished capital punishment, and guaranteed religious freedoms to everyone. However, all his reforms were short-lived and didn't last long after his death.

In Germany, during the mid-18th century, the Enlightenment movement was questioned and critiqued. Events in Europe such as the Seven Years War and the partition of Poland, as well as the American Revolution in North America, led to people abandoning the rationality of Enlightenment for emotionality. Reason was no longer valued, and passion took its place. Philosophers and artists such as Johann Georg Hamann and Johann Wolfgang von Goethe started exploring human emotions. Their goal was to capture their audience by evoking strong feelings such as terror or passion, even if it meant using violence. In such a manner, Goethe's novel *The Sorrows of Young Werther*, first published in 1774, describes the tortures of an unrequited love that eventually leads to suicide.

The Enlightenment failed due to the absolutistic power of the German rulers, but if nothing else, it opened the path for the radical change that was coming from the west: the French Revolution and Napoleon Bonaparte. At the end of the 18th century, Germany was divided into a myriad of small kingdoms that swore allegiance to either Austria or Prussia. There was never a chance for Germany to recover from the Thirty Years' War because the dynastic struggle between the Hohenzollerns and the Habsburgs took hold. The Holy Roman Empire pulled itself apart by proving to the German rulers it offered no protection from outside or inside conflicts. The empire's medieval institutions became obsolete as each ruler set up the administration of his own principality. Germany wasn't prepared for the events of the next century, and the revolution that followed brought dramatic changes.

Chapter 8 – Napoleon and the Revolution in Germany

Portrait of Napoleon Bonaparte
https://en.wikipedia.org/wiki/File:Jacques-Louis_David_-
_The_Emperor_Napoleon_in_His_Study_at_the_Tuileries_-_Google_Art_Project.jpg

In 1848, Europe was shaken by a series of revolutions that flooded the continent like a wave. In February, the revolutions started in France, with the intention of setting up the Second Republic. By springtime, all the major powers experienced political upheaval. The revolution occurred spontaneously in each country rather than as a coordinated effort among the people. The simple spread of the news was enough to influence over fifty countries to successfully bring down monarchical rule in Europe. In Germany, the revolution started in March 1848 when radical liberals and nationalists organized mass demonstrations to bring down their absolutist rulers. German cities transformed from centers of trade, art, and culture to battlefields where street violence held sway.

But the origin of the revolutions of 1848 goes back to the French Revolution of 1792. The Enlightenment inspired people to bring down the monarchy, but consequences that no one could foresee shook Europe's political and social system. The Napoleonic Wars revived nationalism in Germany, especially after the dissolution of the Holy Roman Empire in 1806. After Napoleon's defeat in 1815, the people's efforts and dreams of a republic were smashed when the great powers of the world met in Vienna and formed an alliance to balance the continent's political scene. The monarchs proved they still held all the power and suppressed liberal political agitations around their kingdoms. However, the people continued to dream, and their anger culminated in the spring of 1848. Revolts spontaneously broke out across Europe, and the streets of all the main cities were flooded with people who demanded social and political reforms.

Revolution in France and Its Influence on Germany

The French Revolution lasted from 1789 until 1799. It brought the monarchy down and changed the lives of citizens of France forever. The French people and their fight for freedom from the outdated feudal system inspired the whole of Europe. Revolution spread around the continent like a wildfire, but nowhere did it make an impact like it did in Germany. There, the revolution not only ended the monarchic rule but also brought down the political system that was in place for over 1,000 years—the Holy Roman Empire. While the French Revolution was still in its early years, the Holy Roman Emperor Leopold II decided not to meddle but to observe the situation. He was hoping to turn the revolution to his advantage by using the unrest in neighboring France to solve the age-old struggle between the Habsburg dynasty and the French Crown.

Prussia, another French neighbor, also failed to react to the revolution, as it was busy prospering from yet another partition of Poland. However, it became obvious to the German rulers that if they sat idle, they could lose their thrones, too. Emperor Leopold also had a personal interest in the French Revolution since Queen Marie Antoinette was his sister, and he was afraid something terrible would happen to her. This prompted him to make an alliance with Prussian King Friedrich Wilhelm II, and together, the two German rulers issued the Declaration of Pillnitz. In it, they warned the French revolutionaries that if any harm was done to the French royal family, they would suffer the consequences. But this decree was received as an open threat, and the French did not respond well. The tensions between Austria and the revolutionaries culminated in 1792. The French Revolutionary Assembly declared war on Austria, but at that point, the army of France was in disarray. The revolutionaries had gotten rid of the aristocracy, and there were no capable officers left to lead the army. During their first attack on the Austrian Netherlands, the French soldiers deserted, and the attack itself was a disaster. Before the revolutionaries could retreat and reorganize, the Prussian army invaded France in June of 1792.

But the Prussian general, the Duke of Brunswick, didn't even attempt to appease the situation in France. After taking some of the major fortresses, he issued a decree that turned out to be yet another threat. He repeated the words of Leopold II and demanded that the French king be restored to the throne. Brunswick failed to break the will of the revolutionaries. He only deepened their anger. Prussian support for the monarchy only pushed them to embrace revolutionary ideals, which resulted in the execution of French King Louis XVI and his wife Marie Antoinette in 1793. The execution was certainly provoked by threats made by the German rulers, but it didn't solve anything. In fact, Spain and Portugal realized the dangers of the French Revolution and its influence on Europe and joined Austria and Prussia against France. Since Britain and the Dutch Republic failed to respond to the revolutionaries' pleas, France declared war on them. Cataclysmic struggle was about to break out in Europe, and it would transform the continent through the series of conflicts known as the French Revolutionary Wars.

Many recruits joined the French army as the revolutionary government gained the support of the people, but it still wasn't enough to pose a serious threat to the allied monarchies. During the early campaigns, France suffered heavy losses, and the people who once supported the revolution started rethinking their choices. In truth, all the French army lacked was experience. They had no capable leadership, and all the soldiers recruited had never seen the battlefield before. But after a year of conflict, the French army started winning and even expelling the Allied forces from their territory. By 1794, the French army was ready to go into the offensive and invaded Italy and Spain. Soon, Belgium was overrun, and the Rhineland lost some of its territories, too. In less than a year, the Netherlands was conquered, and the French established the Batavian Republic in its territories. The French victory was sudden and dramatic, and it prompted Prussia and Portugal to retreat from the conflict and the alliance.

Austria was now weakened and an easy target for France. In 1796, the assault was launched when two French armies crossed the Rhine while a third came from the south, where a young military officer named Napoleon Bonaparte led his soldiers through Italy. The goal of the three armies was to meet in Austria and together take Vienna. Austrian military commander and son of Emperor

Leopold II, Archduke Charles managed to defeat the French who were invading from the Rhine. But Napoleon continued his efforts in Italy, where he took the city Mantua. There, he accepted the surrender of the Austrian armies, and the path across the Alps was now open to him. Instead of allowing him to cross, the Austrians sued for peace and accepted humiliating terms. The Treaty of Campo Formio (1797) forced the Austrians to surrender Belgium and Northern Italy, while the Republic of Venice was divided between France and Austria. However, this treaty failed to provide peace, and the conflict was soon renewed.

In the meantime, Napoleon displayed his ambitions to seize power, and the revolutionary French Government was happy to see him gone on his exotic Egyptian campaign. His absence allowed France to make political decisions that would reshape Europe. In Switzerland, the French established another puppet government and named it the Helvetic Republic. In Italy, the French turned their attention to Rome. They deposed Pope Pius VI and established a pro-revolutionary republic in the Eternal City. As a response to these French movements, a second alliance was established between Austria, Britain, and Russia. In 1799, they launched their attack on France. The alliance was doing well in the early conflicts, with Russia taking French possessions in Italy and Austria fighting off the French army and driving it back across the Rhine. But it was the internal conflict among the members of the alliance that determined the end of the war. The Russians retreated because they couldn't reach an agreement with Austria about the conquered territories. Napoleon returned from Egypt and realized his ambitions by proclaiming himself the First Consul, head of the French government. Angered by the political development in Europe, he wanted to retaliate for the second coalition's meddling. Napoleon led an offensive.

The Napoleonic Wars and the End of the Holy Roman Empire

The French Empire at its height in 1812 and its allies (red)

Alexander Altenhof, CC BY-SA 3.0 <https://creativecommons.org/licenses/by-sa/3.0>, via Wikimedia Commons https://commons.wikimedia.org/wiki/File:Europe_1812_map_en.png

Napoleon renewed his campaigns in Italy in 1800. He was successful and changed the course of the war with the victory at the Battle of Marengo when he drove the Austrian army across the Alps. After the victory at the Battle of Hohenlinden in Germany, Napoleon took his army to seize Vienna. Napoleon's victories cause the second coalition to shatter and the Habsburgs to capitulate. With the Treaty of Luneville, signed in 1801, the Austrians were forced to cede the German territories across the Rhine to the French. They also recognized the French client republics in the Netherlands and Italy. After the victory, Napoleon changed his politics, turning from a revolutionary commander into an absolutist. He crowned himself emperor in December of 1804 and revealed his ambitions to conquer Europe. The violent Napoleonic Wars (1803–1815) would devastate the continent in the next decade.

Since the Treaty of Luneville granted German territories to France, the Holy Roman Emperor Francis II (1768–1835) had to come up with a way to compensate the German princes who were forced to cede their lands. To do this, the emperor issued the

Principal Resolution of the Imperial Deputation, by which imperial and ecclesiastical lands were granted to the princes who lost their land in Rhineland. The result was the loss of forty-two imperial cities, which became private possessions of the German princes. But along with the transfer of territory, other effects of the Imperial Deputation were also massive shifts of allegiance. Several German states independently made an alliance with France, which only sped up the dissolution of the Holy Roman Empire.

This shift of alliances made Austria nervous, and the third coalition against France was formed in 1805. The signing parties were Austria, Portugal, Britain, and Russia. However, Napoleon's experience as a military leader proved to be crucial. Although outnumbered, his armies managed to inflict a series of defeats on the coalition. Britain was the only signing party that had some success against the French, mainly because of its dominance in naval battles. At Trafalgar, the French navy suffered a defeat, but in Germany, the French army proved their might on the battlefields. After the victory at the southern German city of Ulm, Napoleon led his army against the allied Austrians and Russians. In December 1805, in the Battle at Austerlitz, the French army won such a decisive victory that the Austrians were forced to back out of the war entirely and sign a treaty. The Treaty of Pressburg detailed the land Austria was to cede to Napoleon's German allies, as well as the war reparations they should pay. The Habsburg Monarchy was ruined by this treaty: it was the last nail in the 1,000-year governance of the Holy Roman Empire over Germany.

By 1806, Napoleon had already signed an official alliance with sixteen German principalities, including Baden, Hesse-Darmstadt, and Saxony. These principalities officially left the Holy Roman Empire and formed what is known as the Confederation of the Rhine (Rheinbund). The territories of the German principalities that signed the alliance were to serve as the buffer zone between France and the Habsburg Monarchy and its coalition. In time, major principalities such as Saxony, Bavaria, and Württemberg were granted the status of kingdoms by the French emperor. Considering these events and the threat that Napoleon posed to the Holy Roman Empire, Francis II officially abdicated as emperor on August 6, 1806. The formal dissolution of the Holy Roman Empire took place on the same day. The rest of the German principalities felt abandoned, and needing protection, they felt pressured to join France and the Confederation of the Rhine. King Francis II continued to rule Austria. Together with Prussia, Swedish Pomerania, and Danish Holstein, he continued to defy Napoleon's ambitions to conquer Europe.

A new coalition was formed in 1806 between Prussia, Britain, Russia, Sweden, and Saxony, which, in the meantime, had left the Confederation of the Rhine. But over the next two years, the coalition was unable to thwart Napoleon's plan to rule Europe. The French emperor inflicted a series of defeats on his enemies. In October 1806, he took Berlin and occupied East Prussia, making a base there which would be later used to launch an attack on Russia. In June 1807, the Russians capitulated and signed the Treaty of Tilsit. France got half of Prussia, which was to become Napoleon's Kingdom of Westphalia.

The division among the German states was best depicted in 1809 during the conflict between Napoleon's armies and those of the fifth coalition. The Confederation of the Rhine was still effective, but the only support Napoleon received during this conflict with Austria and Britain came from Bavaria. The rest of the states tried to remain neutral. However, Napoleon once again displayed his dominion on the battlefield. The decisive battle occurred at Wagram, just outside of Vienna, where around 300,000 soldiers clashed. Austria capitulated, and the Treaty of Schönbrunn was signed, by which the Habsburg Monarchy ceded its Adriatic ports—Galicia, as well as Carinthia and Carniola. Francis II was also forced to agree he would implement an embargo on British goods and recognize Napoleon's brother, Jérôme Bonaparte, as the king of Spain.

The Napoleonic Wars divided Germany, as each state independently gave allegiance to whomever they wanted. However, this situation had an unexpected consequence among the people of Prussia, Austria, and Bavaria: they realized they were all one people, and the sense of German nationalism started growing. The newly-acquired territories of France were populated by German people who resented their new status. The citizens of the Kingdom of Westphalia raised rebellions in their attempt to rejoin their Prussian relatives, and other German territories showed unity against the French overlordship. By the time the sixth coalition was formed in 1812, German people everywhere were united against Napoleon's rule. At that time, Napoleon was in Russia, where he suffered a disastrous defeat. On his way back, with his armies heavily decimated, Napoleon was forced to confront the sixth coalition, made up of Austria, Britain, Russia, Sweden, and Prussia.

The largest battle in Europe before World War I happened in October of 1813. It involved over half a million troops, and it is remembered by the title the Battle of Nations or the Battle of Leipzig. The late 19th-century nationalists grasped the opportunity to celebrate this battle as the romanticized struggle of the German people to expel their French oppressors. But in their celebration, the nationalists decided to remain silent about the fact that Napoleon's troops were aided by his German allies from the Confederation of the Rhine. Nevertheless, the sixth confederation's army won the decisive Battle of Leipzig and pushed the French back over the Rhine. Bavaria, Saxony, and Württemberg switched sides and helped the coalition invade France, where Napoleon was overthrown and the royal Bourbon family was restored. The Confederation of the Rhine collapsed once Russia invaded East Prussia, or the Kingdom of Westphalia. After the battle, most of the confederation members joined the coalition and took part in the Congress of Vienna, during which the borders of European countries were redrawn. In 1815, the German Confederation was born, replacing Napoleon's Confederation of the Rhine. This was not yet Germany as a single state, but the time of its unification was approaching.

The German Confederation was composed of thirty-eight sovereign states and four free cities, all the wreckage that was left after the dissolution of the Holy Roman Empire. They were governed by the Austrian emperor who, in the case of Germany, served in the role of president. Still, each state had a level of individuality, and its representatives met only once a year in Frankfurt. The Austrian representative would also attend the meeting to discuss any major problems the confederation might have. The German Confederation was a very conservative environment that tried to expel all the French revolutionary influences and liberal ideas. The German Confederation issued several very oppressive pieces of legislation with the intention of preventing the rise of the populace. The press was censored, leaving the people of Germany largely unaware of the liberal tides that were sweeping through Europe. In 1820, Austria, Prussia, and Russia formed the Holy Alliance to preserve autocracy within the German Confederation and allow the monarch to have tight control over these lands.

The Revolution of 1848 in Germany

Since the Congress of Vienna in 1815, the German Confederation had been stable and prosperous under its conservative rule. However, by 1830, the people realized that stability was an illusion, and tension grew once more in Central Europe. Threatened by revolutions, the monarchs of Austria, Prussia, and Russia met in secrecy to form yet another Holy Alliance. The meeting took place in Berlin in 1833, and the alliance's goals of preserving the monarchic rule were reaffirmed. France and Belgium had already deposed their monarchs in 1830, and Poland was on the verge of rebellion. The Holy Alliance managed to subdue the revolutionary sentiment that was rising in its member's countries, but this was only a temporary solution. When, in 1848, the revolutionary current from France reached Germany, the alliance was unable to prevent the uprising. The nationalism and liberal ideas from the rest of Europe reached the German populace, and they expressed revolt against the conservative government that ruled them. The first signs of the revolution happened in March of 1848 when riots broke out in several German cities. The people demanded political and social reforms, but they, too, were divided between the radicals, influenced by French revolutionaries, and the liberals, who were mostly educated individuals.

The era before the revolution of 1848 was known as the Vormärz era, the German romanticism which brought forth nationalism. The pan-German anthem "Das Lied der Deutschen" (The Song of the Germans) was written in 1841, and it evoked a nationalistic spirit and ideas among the people. Famous German poet Heinrich Heine wrote lyric poetry filled with images that stirred national passion, although the Nazis later found his persona to be inadequate, as he was originally Jewish. These nationalistic ideas inspired the youth of Germany, who formed clubs that gathered people of the same opinions. Youth clubs sprouted all over Germany, rising from both sports clubs and university fraternities (known as Burschenschaften in Germany), and they promoted liberal and nationalistic ideas. The government tried to prohibit the activities of youth clubs by issuing repressive edicts and decrees to limit the spread of nationalistic and liberal thinking. Membership in Burschenschaften was made illegal, and universities had to employ inspectors who would monitor the activities of students and professors.

The first mass protest organized to call for a unified Germany took place in 1832. It is known today as the Hambacher Fest, an event that gathered around 30,000 students, professors, politicians, and workers demanding a unified government and freedom for citizens. This protest didn't achieve much, but it was a symbol of the growing influence of liberalism and nationalism and a prelude to the March Revolution of 1848, wherein the spirit of Hambacher Fest grasped the whole of Germany. The citizens' discontent grew with each passing year, so when the revolutionary wave came from France, the German populace was already on the verge, ready to take up the streets and fight for the new order. The German middle class formed mobs all over the German cities, demanding freedom of the press, the unification of the state, and the formation of a parliament. They were quickly joined by factory workers and farmers, who were hit hard by the rapid industrialization taking place.

Amid the revolution, which spread throughout Europe, the working class was exposed to the writings of radical left socialists such as Karl Heinrich Marx (1818–1883), who had just published *The Communist Manifesto*. Marx was trained as a philosopher and a journalist, and his masterworks were written as a call to the working class to pick up arms and fight for their rights. His ideas set the foundation on which modern Communism was raised. He believed that human history could be observed as an ongoing economic and social struggle. His vision of the future was one in which production and development are controlled by the workers themselves, who would, in time, build a stateless and classless society. Marx's *Manifesto* and his persona remained obscure during the revolution of 1848, but after his death, his ideas would shape the future of Germany. Karl Marx would have a tremendous influence on the whole world, for good or for bad.

When the revolution in France turned into a coup that removed King Louis-Philippe, the German people saw the change that the masses can bring. By February, they had already issued a resolution that demanded a constitution. The stage was set for the March Revolution, and smaller protests occurred early in Baden, the Duchy of Hesse, the Duchy of Nassau, and the Kingdom of Württemberg. The rulers of the German Confederation were caught off guard by the spontaneous protests that were popping up in their territories. To appease the people, they made various concessions, but in Baden, violence erupted. The ducal army attacked the republican demonstrators, and this violence would soon spread throughout Germany. The revolutionaries prepared, raising a republican militia led by Friedrich Hecker (1811-1881). They were ready to confront the soldiers of Baden and Hesse, and the first conflict came on April 20, 1848, in the Black Forest. The aristocratic army defeated the revolutionaries, but with heavy losses. Disappointed, Hecker emigrated to America, where he later became the commander of a Union regiment during the American Civil War.

In Berlin, the capital of Prussia, which was a conservatively autocratic kingdom, the protesters dared to take to the streets. They demanded concession from King Friedrich Wilhelm IV (1795-1861), who responded that he would give them a constitution, parliament, and the freedom of speech and press. But he didn't stop there. Inspired by the revolution, the Prussian king promised he would help his people unite Germany into one nation and state. But the people believed their king's promises were empty and continued with protests. The situation in Berlin culminated when one of the anxious Prussian soldiers guarding the barricades fired at the angry mob. By March 18, the Prussian capital became a war zone. The conflict lasted for three days, and hundreds of protestors were killed by Prussian soldiers. In the end, King Friedrich Wilhelm went out on the streets of Berlin to appease the situation. He reaffirmed his intentions of concessions and visited the graves of the fallen protestors who had died during the conflict.

In Austria, Emperor Ferdinand I was shocked by the situation in Germany. Austria was the leader of the German Confederation, and the protests there were aiming at the Habsburg emperor. But it wasn't only Germany that was worrying him—the situation in Austria wasn't good, either. By March, the revolution took to the streets of Vienna, where it raged until July of 1849. The revolution in Austria was sparked by various nationalities that were part of the Habsburg Monarchy and sought autonomy: Slovaks, Serbs, Croats, Hungarians, Poles, Czechs, Italians, and Romanians. The threat to the Habsburg emperor came from two sides: the German

Confederation and his empire. Pressured, Ferdinand I reluctantly exiled his favorite politician and chancellor, Klemens von Metternich, who had kept the conservative spirit in both Austria and the German Confederation and led the politics of central Europe for three decades. However, the resignation and exile of the Austrian chancellor to England weren't enough for the people. Soon, the emperor was forced to abdicate and name his nephew, Franz Joseph (1830-1916), as his successor.

In Frankfurt, a new National Assembly emerged and replaced the German Confederation, taking over its duties. The National Assembly met in Frankfurt and was accordingly named the Frankfurt Parliament. Elections followed, and the parliament swelled up to 586 delegates, all chosen from the rows of liberal intellectuals. The chair of the parliament was taken up by the Hessian statesman, Heinrich von Gagern, and the parliament immediately started working on the constitution. The constitution intended to establish the foundations for a unified nation-state of Germany with a single parliament. But the first difficulty emerged almost immediately as the delegates argued whether to include Austria in the new, united Germany or leave it out. The problem arose when some of the delegates pointed out that Austria was a multinational empire, filled with Slavs, Italians, and Romanians, and as such, it wouldn't fit into a new state that was based on cultural, lingual, and national unity. The argument lasted for months until they reached the resolution that Austria should not be admitted into the new state but should be bound to it by a special treaty. When even after a year the Frankfurt Parliament failed to yield a constitution, it started losing prestige among the German populace. France, Russia, and other European forces didn't even recognize the legitimacy of this parliament, while Austria and Prussia completely ignored it. When the parliament finally released its constitution in March 1849, it barely passed the vote and was recognized only by some of the minor states of the German Confederation. The major European powers refused to do so.

When the revolution was only starting in Prussia, King Friedrich Wilhelm IV was on the side of the people and even promised them a constitution. However, he soon realized, by the example of the German Confederation, that the political tide in Europe was very much against the radical ideas of the revolutionists. Therefore, when the people offered him the crown (as they were proud to have a king who would give them a constitution), Friedrich declined it, calling it a crown made of mud and clay. The Prussian king turned to autocracy once more. In Frankfurt, the parliament fell apart, and the revolution dissolved into separate movements across the Confederation. The most radical leftists continued to meet and eventually tried to organize their parliament in Stuttgart, but they were soon chased away by the Royal Dragoons of the Kingdom of Württemberg. The fragmented revolution allowed German princes to assert their dominion once more, and the demonstrations were often stifled by ruthless violence. In Stuttgart, where the leftovers of the National Assembly exiled the Duke of Baden, the Prussian army stormed the demonstrators acting on behalf of the German Confederation. In Saxony, the conflict culminated in remarkable proportions when the military, called by King Friedrich Augustus, joined the protesters. The king was forced to call on the Prussian army to quell the uprising, and tensions escalated. The crowd was angry and grew more violent with each passing day, finally forcing Friedrich Augustus into the fortified armory. The protesters tried to enter the armory, but the royal guard fired at them, and the City of Dresden became a war zone. The revolutionary protesters barricaded themselves in the city, expecting the Prussian army. They even organized a provisional government that would manage the conflict and eventually force their monarch to accept the liberal reforms guaranteed by the Frankfurt constitution. The Prussian and Saxon troops united against the protesters, and the street fighting that followed was ruthless and brutal. By May 9, no revolutionary forces remained in the city. The majority were slaughtered, but some managed to escape the country and find refuge in neighboring countries, as well as America. Among them was famous composer Richard Wagner, who fled to Switzerland. The conflict in Saxony is remembered as the May Uprising.

By June 1849, the revolution was over. The monarch managed to tighten the conservative yolk on the population of Germany. The leaders of the revolution were either dead or imprisoned, the German Confederation was back, and the assembly returned to the conservative vision of the exiled chancellor Metternich. The disappointed liberals and nationalists who survived the revolutionary year were now mockingly called the Forty-Eighters, and they collectively emigrated to the United States. The failure of the March Revolution changed the course of Germany's history. Instead of unifying the nation, the powerful states of Austria and Prussia resumed their struggle for dominion over the German Confederation. The peace and the prospect of unity were doomed, and the nation-state, the dream of the revolutionaries, would be born out of future bloodshed.

Chapter 9 – The Many Wars and the Unification

In 1850, after the revolution, Prussian King Friedrich Wilhelm IV finally issued a constitution. However, it was a conservative document supporting his autocracy. He did give some liberal freedoms to the citizens and formed a Prussian Parliament consisting of the lower house (the Landtag) and the upper house (the Herrenhaus). The delegates of the Landtag were to be elected, but the voters were not equal. The members who paid higher taxes held higher voting powers. The members of the Herrenhaus were appointed by the king himself. The king also had complete authority over the cabinets of the ministers and the civil service and army. But the king suffered a stroke in 1857, and Prussia fell under the regency of his younger brother, Wilhelm. By 1861, Wilhelm took the throne as King Wilhelm I.

The German statesman Otto von Bismarck (1815-1898) was appointed as Prussian minister-president and was tasked with unifying Germany under Prussian rule. He served under Wilhelm I (1797-1888), who had succeeded to the Prussian crown a year earlier. A decade before, there was almost war between Prussia and Austria in the autumn crisis of 1850, but Prussia withdrew and suffered a diplomatic defeat. Prussia had weakened greatly, and the only way it could join the major European powers on the political scene was at the head of a unified Germany. Bismarck was no idealist—he understood very well that the new nation-state would have to be born out of major conflict, a war of enormous proportions.

However, the Prussian kingdom had formed a budget commission to lift the state out of the economic crisis that emerged after its defeat by the Austrians. This commission was in Bismarck's way, as it was opposed to waging another expensive war. The army needed to be reorganized, and this endeavor would be extremely costly. Instead, the budget commission thought it would be much wiser to implement liberal social reforms. Bismarck confronted the commission and, in his speech, stressed the need for Prussia's military power to unite Germany. He planned to exclude Austria from unification, and the only possible way to do it was through major conflict. In the next few decades, this Prussian politician would repeatedly demonstrate his will to wage war to achieve his ambitions. Parliamentary delegates refused to vote in favor of war, but Bismarck managed to inspire the people and awaken the nationalism and patriotism among them. The people wanted unification with the German Confederation and expressed their single-minded determination. Bismarck further managed to raise the funds for military reforms without the consent of parliament. He ignored their votes and evaded their authority just so he could have his war and unite Germany under Prussia.

But while the budget commission was against the war and military reforms because of their cost, many conservative officers, civil servants, and aristocracy opposed the unification of Germany because they feared that the status of their beloved Prussia would diminish with the union. They also expressed their fears that the Prussian king would be forced to accept liberal reforms under a unified Germany. Bismarck agreed that the destiny of Prussia was a concern, but he argued that if Germany was unified under their ruler, Prussia would emerge as the greatest European power. During the 1850s, Prussia was marginalized by other European powers such as France and Britain, who had dominated the Crimean War (1854–1855) against Russia. Bismarck pointed this out and argued that Prussia had to return to the political scene of Europe immediately if it wished to continue existing. Otherwise, it represented a very attractive war prey with its rich coal mines and iron industry.

The war between Prussia and Austria erupted in 1866, two years after the Second Schleswig War fought between Denmark and the united forces of Prussia and Austria. The reason behind the conflict in 1866 was that the Austrian Empire disputed with the German Confederation about the Danish territories conquered during the earlier war. The Prussians accused Austria of breaking the settlement that followed the Second Schleswig War and then invaded Holstein. In response to the Prussian accusations, the German Confederation authorized the mobilization of troops to counter the invasion. Bismarck was not intimidated; he even wished for war and declared the Confederation dissolved. Most of the German states joined the Austrian side in the conflict, while Prussia had the support of minor northern German states and the Kingdom of Italy. Italy had its reasons for stepping into the conflict with Austria. It hoped for territorial gains—specifically, the Veneto (the area surrounding today's Venice), which was under Austrian control. Europe's major powers stayed out of the conflict.

The Prussians prepared for war even before it was declared, and they had the advantage. While Austria was still mobilizing its troops, the Prussians invaded Saxony and Bohemia. The modernization of the army served Bismarck well, as the new breech-loading rifles overwhelmed the Austrian soldiers. The Austrians suffered their first defeat at Königgrätz, on July 3, 1866, and immediately sued for peace. But Prussia turned against the Austrian allies since Bismarck understood German states wouldn't accept Prussia's dominance easily. By the end of the month, the Hanoverian army was defeated, and the Bavarians were pushed back to the River Main. The Peace of Prague, which ended the conflict between Prussia and Austria, was signed on August 23rd. The war lasted only for seven weeks, but Austria ended up excluded from the future unification of Germany. Prussia emerged as the leading state in the German Confederation, which was immediately dissolved so the Prussians could form a new one. The new alliance, known as the North German Confederation, included twenty-one of the German states, all occupying the territories north of the River Main. The German nationalists welcomed the new Confederation, and Prussia became their only hope of a unified state that would exclude multinational Austria. Prussia annexed Austrian allies such as Nassau, Hesse-Kessel, and Hanover, and forced several other states to join the Northern German Confederation. The position of Prussia changed on the larger European scale, and the kingdom was back in the political game of central Europe. Bismarck remained the minister-president and, as such, dominated not only Prussian but also the politics of the new Confederation.

The Franco-Prussian War

Prussia's return to the political scene of Europe alarmed France. France felt threatened not only by the fact that the Hohenzollerns had gained control over all of Germany but also by their military power. Napoleon III (1808–1873) understood very well that French influence on the southern German states was the cause of Bismarck's turn towards them. To integrate these southern territories into his new Confederation, Bismarck would have to wage war against Germany's centuries-old enemy, France. But first, the Prussian minister-president ensured that other European powers wouldn't meddle in the conflict. His diplomatic skills proved to be great, as he managed to persuade Russia and Great Britain to stay out of the war. But he needed a reason to declare the war on France, and the opportunity presented itself in Spain. The Spanish throne had been vacant since the revolution in 1868 and was now being offered to the cousin of the Prussian king, Prince

Leopold of the Hohenzollern-Sigmaringen dynasty. If he accepted the Spanish crown, France would be surrounded by territories controlled by Prussia, and it had to act immediately. Napoleon III first tried diplomacy, sending his trusted ambassador Vincente Benedetti to meet with Wilhelm I to demand the refusal of the Spanish crown. The Prussian king agreed to the French demands, as he wasn't willing to participate in yet another military conflict. However, France wasn't satisfied. Napoleon III insisted that Wilhelm I should promise that no Hohenzollern would ever occupy the Spanish throne. He even asked that an official apology be issued by the Prussian king, but he only managed to insult Wilhelm I, who rejected all of France's demands. This situation was the perfect opportunity Bismark needed to proclaim war on France. Indulging in shrewd politics, he issued Ems Dispatch, a document that described the French-Prussian correspondence. Bismarck's version of the correspondence was much different than the original. He changed several sentences to insult France and inspire anti-French sentiment among Germans. The reaction was immediate, as France declared war on Prussia on July 19, 1870.

Prussia had the full support of the whole north German Confederation as well as the south German states, who allied with Prussia against France. Just as in the previous war with Austria, Prussia mobilized its army quickly, while France took its time. The result was the invasion of France under the supreme command of King Wilhelm I. But it wasn't easy to breach the French border, and it took several weeks for Prussia to gain the upper hand. On August 2nd, the French army was overwhelmed and defeated on several fronts. The following weeks saw Prussian victories at Weissenburg, Wörth, and Spichern, forcing Napoleon III to change the commanding officer in the middle of the conflict. The newly-appointed Marshal François-Achille Bazaine couldn't break the Prussian advance and was forced to retreat to the City of Metz, a fortified stronghold close to the French-German border. Prussians besieged the city, but Napoleon III personally led the newly-built army to relieve the city and his commanding officer Bazaine. Hearing of the approaching French army, the Prussians split. While one part of their forces kept Metz under pressure, the second part ambushed Napoleon at Beaumont on August 30th. The defeat the French suffered made them retreat and regroup so they could mount a defense for the upcoming decisive battle.

Outside the French town Sedan, on September 1, 1870, the German and French forces clashed in battle. The exhausted French forces were desperate and tried to break out of Sedan so they wouldn't get trapped and besieged, just like at Metz. They moved towards the city of La Moncelle, which was in a strategically better position for defense. Saxon and Prussian troops approached the city and found it easy to enter. The fighting continued on the city streets. Feeling overwhelmed, the French general ordered a retreat, but one of his officers, Emmanuel de Wimpffen, decided to disregard the order and launch an offensive. He was successful against the Saxon troops, but his rally was short-lived, as the Prussian and Bavarian troops came to help their allies. The situation was hopeless for France, and when Napoleon arrived at the battle scene on the evening of September 1, he called off the French attempts at a counterattack. The French suffered heavy losses—around 17,000 soldiers were killed, almost double the German losses. The next day, the French emperor surrendered and was taken into custody. The German victory at La Moncelle caused the collapse of France's Second Empire. However, the provisional government in Paris continued to wage war with Prussia for another five months. In turn, the Prussians continued towards Paris and besieged it. Parisians endured constant shelling as well as bombardment and finally surrendered on January 19, 1871.

Germany Unified

Europe after the war

In Germany, the nationalism spirit sparked by Bismarck's politics grasped the populace even stronger as they celebrated the glorious victory of King Wilhelm I. But the biggest event in history for Germany occurred on French soil: Wilhelm I was crowned emperor of unified Germany on January 18th, in the Versailles' Hall of Mirrors in Paris. The new empire, or the so-called Second Reich, came into existence just as Otto von Bismarck predicted—from bloodshed. Baden, Württemberg, and Bavaria joined the North German Confederation, and Germany was finally unified, but it was ruled by the iron fist of Prussia. The new monarchical empire Wilhelm I created included all the German states of the previous German Confederation, excluding Austria as well as the tiny states of Luxembourg and Liechtenstein, which decided to remain neutral.

The newly-formed German Empire, or the Kaiserreich, was an autocratic state with a constitution issued in 1871 that ensured Prussian domination. Bismarck, who took up the role of chancellor, granted some democratic concessions to keep the liberals at peace.

The bicameral parliament was founded with a lower house (Reichstag) whose delegates had to be elected. He also allowed the formation of political parties, but he was careful to preserve the conservative spirit of the North German Confederation. If the political parties wanted to propose legislation, they had to be approved by the Bundesrat, a federal council under the control of German princes, who could block all liberal reforms. But Prussia, as the dominant force of the empire, was the only state with veto powers within Bundesrat. The constitution guaranteed that only fourteen votes were enough to block a constitutional change, and Prussia alone had seventeen delegates. The emperor had all the executive power, and Bismarck, his chancellor, had it, too. According to the new constitution, the chancellor was obliged to oversee all the aspects of the government, and the authority to enact legislation lay with him. Bismarck made sure that he created an imperial structure with a constitution to safeguard these institutions and Prussian dominion. Although the imperial constitution had traces of democratic ideals, it completely supported and ensured the authoritarian nature of united Germany.

France's Third Republic signed a settlement with the German Empire on May 10, 1871, in Frankfurt. The hostilities officially ended, and France was forced to cede the territories of Alsace and Lorraine. It also had to agree to stay under German occupation until it paid the war indemnity of approximately five billion francs. While united Germany celebrated its victory over France, these events paved the road for future European conflicts, from which it would emerge as the global power. Germany's and Prussia's astonishing climb to power was a warning for the rest of Europe, which finally realized the consequences of allowing Prussia to pursue its militaristic ambitions.

Imperial Germany wasn't only among the greatest European powers in military terms. It also managed to surpass Britain in industrial and economic development. Iron and coal were mined to produce machines, which were transported easily all over the empire with the newly-built railroad system. French Alsace and Lorraine were also industrial centers, and now they added to Germany's already mighty industry. With economic gains came the prosperity of the people. The populace of the empire increased, transforming towns into cities and cities into metropolitan areas. Britain had dominated the industrial scene of Europe since the early 18th century, and now Germany became a worthy rival. The German exports of goods tripled in the decades that followed the unification. At the turn of the century, Germany was quickly rising to become a global economic power, second only to the United States.

Bismarck succeeded in bringing about the German Empire, but he continued to work tirelessly to ensure his vision of a nation-state was completely fulfilled. The people still needed to be unified, and the empire needed to be firmly centralized, with Prussia at its helm. He needed to maintain the conservative nature of the state, and to do this, he needed to stop religious activism, which had spread through the German Catholic minority. His efforts in the field of religion are known as the Kulturkampf. It all started in 1864 when Pope Pius IX (1792–1878) called on the Catholics of Europe to fight against the secular nature of society. The pope opposed state-sponsored education and civil marriages, and in 1871, he issued a declaration that claimed the pope was always right when it came to religious matters. This angered Bismarck, and in 1872, he expelled the Jesuits from Prussia. The May Law he issued the same year gave the state the right to train and appoint all the clergy in Germany. He closed Catholic seminaries and arrested those who either openly opposed him or broke the new law. Furthermore, he confiscated all the church properties and heavily regulated the activities of the Catholic clergy. Pope Pius proclaimed Bismarck's May Law invalid and called on the German Catholics to oppose the official religious persecution. The result of the May Law was the formation of the Catholic Center Party in the south of Germany. But Catholics from all over the empire joined this political party to support it and officially voice their opposition to the law. Bismarck thought of Catholicism as an obstacle to Germany's prosperity. Catholics were extremely loyal to the church instead of to the united nation-state, and the chancellor wouldn't allow it.

But the repression measures he implemented only served to strengthen the resolve of his enemies. Pressed by other matters of the state, Bismarck abandoned his Kulturkampf. He joined the Catholic Center Party so they could more effectively fight the growing socialism within Germany. The first workers' party in Germany was founded in 1863 by Ferdinand Lassalle, a Forty-Eighter who had just been released from prison, where he had served time for his involvement in the revolution. The name of the party was the General German Workers' Association (or ADAV, shortened from its original German name). But this party wasn't the only one. Marxists Wilhelm Liebknecht and August Bebel founded the Social Democratic Workers' Party of Germany (SDAP) in 1869. Although ADAV and SDAP started as bitter enemies with different socialist ideas and programs, they agreed to convene in the meeting organized in May of 1875 to discuss the possibility of unification. This would greatly help plan the future of the workers in Germany. The newly founded party was named the Socialist Workers' Party of Germany (SAPD). It grew rapidly, and with the new members came new ideas and plans. The party was forced to change its name to the Social Democratic Party of Germany (SDP) when its ideology changed and its members started demanding a republican government.

In 1878, there were a few attempts to assassinate Emperor Wilhelm, and while the Socialists took no part in them, Bismarck took the opportunity to accuse them and eventually crush their influence in Germany. He issued a set of laws, named Anti-Socialist Laws, to eradicate socialism. The first law forbade the organizations which, through their activities, sought to overthrow the established state and social order. He even pointed out that this included Social Democratic, Socialist, or Communist political parties. He also employed state militia to break up any workers' assembly or political gatherings of the said parties. The radical newspapers were also shut down to suppress the spread of Socialist ideology.

But just as with the Catholics, Bismarck's ideas to stop German socialism failed. The leaders of various organizations went into hiding, and the Socialist Party continued to grow, with new members joining each day. Seeing that it was impossible to suppress socialism, the chancellor changed the tactic. He issued a series of progressive social programs with which he tried to anticipate the Socialist demands. The first such program came in 1881, and it intended to prevent accidents in the workplace for miners and industrial workers. In 1883, a national healthcare system was introduced in Germany, as well as a program to help disabled people. In 1887, a retirement pension system was set up, and with it, Germany emerged as a state with the most progressive social system in the entire world. Even though Bismarck tried to suppress socialism in his country, the welfare programs he introduced ended up being by far more progressive than the ones in France or Britain.

Aside from fighting against religious activism and socialism, Bismarck had his ideology to promote. He still felt the need to unite the people into one single nation and to prevent the old principalities from demanding autonomy. He had yet to create one German national spirit which would inspire the people to fight for the common goals of the state. To do this, Bismarck came up with the idea of unique policies that would foster national unity, commonly known as Germanization. He was keen to eradicate multiculturalism in Germany by opening various national institutions. To manage these new institutions, Germany needed a new set of laws. They came in 1900 in the shape of a civil code, known as the Bürgerliches Gesetzbuch. Many new national institutions were there to promote cultural nationalism, and they required the use of the German language in all aspects of life. Education and government also demanded strict use of German, and consequently, the ethnic minorities of Germany were assimilated. Bismarck even went so far as to organize a forced relocation of Poles. In 1885, he wanted to colonize the areas previously conquered from Poland with ethnic Germans. In total, 20,000 individuals of Polish descent were exiled to Russia. The Poles' resistance and soon pro-Polish political party were organized to oppose Bismarck. As with the Catholics and Socialists, governmental efforts to suppress ideology only resulted in disobedience and defiance.

Bismarck's domestic politics brought many changes to Germany, but they all eventually failed. However, he was more successful in foreign politics. He was aware that France still held a grudge for the loss of territories during the Franco-Prussian War, and he formed international alliances with other European powers as a safeguard. The first such alliance came to be in 1872, and it was called the League of the Three Emperors because it gathered the emperors of Russia, Germany, and Austria under the same military alliance. But this alliance broke up during the Russo-Turkish War (1877–1878), and the German chancellor joined the Austro-Hungarian Empire in a dual alliance against Russia. In 1882, Italy joined the alliance, and through this country, Austria and Germany were linked with Britain and Spain due to the Mediterranean Agreement of 1887.

Chapter 10 – World War I

Scenes from the Great War
https://commons.wikimedia.org/wiki/File:WWImontage.jpg

World War I, a military conflict that destroyed the German Empire, was a demonstration of the horrors various nations could unleash upon each other. It started on July 28, 1914, when Germany was under the rule of Wilhelm II (1859-1941), an authoritarian and bellicose ruler. While he was still a crown prince, Wilhelm fell under Bismarck's influence and, once he succeeded to the throne in 1888, abandoned the progressive politics of his father, Emperor Friedrich III, who ruled for only ninety-nine days and died of throat cancer. Wilhelm II idolized Wilhelm I and wanted to return Germany to the state it was in during the early rule of his grandfather. The young monarch was impatient, and he demanded the war, while Bismarck tried to maintain peace. The clash between Wilhelm II and the Germans' great politician led to a domestic disaster.

Wilhelm wanted to take up a more active role in the politics of Germany and would often clash with Bismarck just to prove his capability to lead the country. He even tried to gain the support of Germany's working class by arguing against Bismarck's Anti-Socialist Laws, but he only managed to anger the aging politician. After another heated argument with his emperor, Bismarck—nicknamed the Iron Chancellor of Germany—resigned in 1890. Kaiser Wilhelm II was resolved to rule the German Empire more personally, and he employed a puppet chancellor. But the emperor's meddling in domestic and foreign politics resulted in a series of crises, the first in 1896. Wilhelm hated the British and rushed to send a telegraph to the president of Transvaal Republic (an internationally recognized republic in South Africa from 1852-1902, settled by the Dutch), congratulating him on the victory against the British. Once the telegram became public, the British were outraged, and the debacle of Wilhelm's politics was known to all European forces.

But Wilhelm resented the policy of avoiding the conflict with Britain implemented earlier by Bismarck, and he started building a fleet—one that would overpower the naval might of King Edward

VII of England. The German population didn't object to building a fleet, as they saw it necessary to protect German colonies and trade interests across the sea. The British were alarmed by Germany's sudden interest in the navy, and the competition began. Both powers were building battleships tirelessly just to keep with each other's pace. The naval race resulted in Britain and France establishing the Entente Cordiale in 1904, an agreement that ended their centuries-old animosity and united them to protect their colonies. As France already had an alliance with Russia, the third power was automatically added to the agreement. The focus of the new alliance was to counter Germany and restore the power balance within Europe.

In 1905, the German emperor created another debacle while visiting Morocco: he held a series of speeches in which he insinuated that he supported Moroccan independence. As this African state was a French protectorate, naturally France had to react and started gearing up for war. However, Germany proposed a conference to resolve the issue, and persuaded by Britain, France agreed to attend. The Algeciras Conference was held in Spain in 1906, and it proved to be a disaster for Germany. France had the support of Britain, Italy, Spain, Russia, and the United States, while Germany had only the Austro-Hungarian Empire by its side. The conference decided to grant control of Morocco to France, and Germany had to suffer an embarrassing political fiasco.

The following year, Britain and Russia signed a convention in St. Petersburg, ending the rivalry between the British Crown and the imperial Romanov Dynasty. Germany was now surrounded by the three greatest allied European powers: France, Britain, and Russia. When the Second Moroccan Crisis came in 1911 and the rebellion against the sultan broke out, Wilhelm seized the opportunity to intervene and challenge Anglo-French control in Africa. He sent a gunboat, the SMS Panther, to help the rebelling Moroccans against the French and the British who came to quell the rebellion. However, the Germans were not powerful enough to fight both armies and had to sue for the end of the crisis. Germany offered recognition of French dominion over Morocco in return for territorial concessions in Congo. With the Treaty of Fes signed on November 4, 1911, the Second Moroccan crisis ended. But the result was not what Wilhelm wanted it to be. Instead of breaking the Anglo-French alliance, his actions managed only to strengthen their opposition to Germany. Although Wilhelm's actions didn't start the global conflict known as World War I, his attempts to meddle in European politics set the stage for it. Alliances were formed, and the relations between the states were so tense that it took just one spark to ignite the war. That spark came from an unexpected place: the Balkan, the silent giant of Europe.

The Start of the War

The rival factions at the start of the war

historicair (French original)Fluteflute & User:Bibi Saint-Pol (English translation), CC BY-SA 2.5 <https://creativecommons.org/licenses/by-sa/2.5>, via Wikimedia Commons https://commons.wikimedia.org/wiki/File:Map_Europe_alliances_1914-en.svg

After centuries of Turkish rule and the struggle to end it, the Balkan region was like a keg of powder waiting to explode. It was populated by ethnic groups that felt extreme hostility towards one another: Slovenes, Croats, Serbs, Romanians, Bulgarians, and Albanians. Europe was entering its era of ardent nationalism and was influenced by great forces, and these ethnic groups wanted to form their own nation-states. But after Ottoman rule, the Balkan was Austro-Hungarian territory, and the signs of individuality coming from the small ethnic groups of the region were a threat to the empire. After Turkey retreated from the Balkans in 1878, Austria-Hungary occupied the province of Bosnia-Herzegovina in hopes that it would prevent a nationalistic uprising. Austria wanted to annex this territory, but Russia, a champion of Slavic spirit, prevented it. However, in 1908, Russia had a change of heart and agreed to the Austrian annex of Bosnia-Herzegovina in exchange for territories in the Mediterranean. But Austria jumped forward and proclaimed the annexation without signing the treaty with Russia. Another ethnic group opposed the annexation, as it believed it had territorial rights within Bosnia, too: the Serbs. The war was about to break, but Germany stood up with its ally, Austria, forcing the Russians and the Serbs to calm their passions.

By 1912, the Ottoman Empire was dying, and to share its former territories, a Balkan league was formed among Bulgaria, Macedonia, Serbia, and Greece. During the First Balkan War (1912–1913), the League of Balkans forced the Turks out of the Balkan region, and with them gone, a dangerous power vacuum formed in the region. European major forces— France, Austria, and Russia—met in London to arrange the post-war settlement. The result was the creation of a new nation, Albania. But this didn't resolve the problem in the Balkans. It only elevated the hostile situation and, to this day, the Balkan Peninsula remains the problematic region of Europe. Bulgaria asked for part of Macedonia, but its meddling in the settlement only sparked another war. The Second Balkan War started in 1913, and Bulgaria lost to allied Serbia, Romania, Greece, and even Turkey. Serbia and Greece divided Macedonia between themselves, and some of the Bulgarian territories near the Black Sea were ceded to Romania. But matters were not settled, as this conflict only stirred the various Balkan ethnic groups to aspire to nationalism.

The event which plunged Europe into conflict occurred on June 28, 1914, in Sarajevo (today's capital of Bosnia and Herzegovina). Gavrilo Princip, a Bosnian nationalist, assassinated the Habsburg Archduke Franz Ferdinand (1863–1914). He was angry that Austria annexed Bosnia and Herzegovina and thought that killing the next in line to the Austro-Hungarian throne would shake the world enough to free his country from the imperial grasp. However, the outcome was much more violent and bloody. A war ensued, one that would, for the first time in human history, be fought between all major political world powers. At the time, the war was simply called "The Great War." The name World War I was given to it only after World War II proved that the world was still not safe from such large-scale conflicts.

Franz Ferdinand wasn't the only victim of the assassination. His wife, Sophie Chotek Ferdinand, was shot too. They were the guests of the provincial governor of Sarajevo, who had invited them to attend a military parade in the city. Gavrilo Princip also wasn't the only assassin. His companions had failed in previous attempts to kill the archduke by bombing his car. But the same day, when Franz Ferdinand was on his way to the hospital to visit those who were hurt in the bombing attempt, his driver made a wrong turn, and Gavrilo approached the car and shot two shots from his pistol. Gavrilo Princip was immediately apprehended, and during the later questioning, he revealed he was a member of the Bosnian nationalistic youth organization "Young Bosnia," which was trained and financed by the Serbian nationalistic group known as "the Black Hand." Even though the Serbian government learned about the assassination plans and made the leaders of the organization call it off, Gavrilo Princip and his co-conspirators continued with the plan. The assassination was supposed to trigger conflict between Austria and Serbia, and the plotters hoped Russia would join and help their Slavic relatives. But the outcome was much worse. The tensions between the Anglo-French alliance and Germany, created by Emperor Wilhelm II, was just waiting for a spark like this to enter into open conflict. Gavrilo Princip and the assassination of Franz Ferdinand were just the sparks the great European forces needed.

Austrians were outraged by the events of June 28th and called for revenge upon the Serbian people, counting on the support of Wilhelm II and their alliance with Germany. Russia was expected to side with Serbia in the conflict, but instead, it consulted with France. Together, they tried to find a peaceful solution to the problem. But, on July 23rd, the Austrians issued an ultimatum to Serbia. This infamous July Ultimatum was filled with humiliating demands the Serbians would surely decline, even if it meant war. The whole world accused Austria of deliberately pushing for war, but they were aware Austria's ally, Germany, was a very powerful military force that they were not prepared to fight at the time. Austria was permitted to send an ultimatum to Serbia. Crown Prince Alexander of Serbia asked Russia for support, but the only thing he managed to get was moral support. The Russians advised him to accept the ultimatum and not risk war. In the end, it seems Serbia accepted all the points of the July Ultimatum except Clause 6, which demanded Austro-Hungarian police operate on Serbian soil. At first, the Austrians were disappointed Serbia accepted the ultimatum, but they saw the rejection of Clause 6 as reason enough to attack. A conference was proposed to solve the issue further, as Europe saw the Serbian's willingness to adhere to the ultimatum, but Austria declined, wishing for war. On July 28th, war was officially declared, and Germany sought a way to back out of the conflict. Wilhelm II reached out to Britain, trying to make a treaty that would bind them to stay neutral, but it was too late. His previous actions had angered Britain, and the proposal was refused.

The Fighting

Early in August of 1914, all the European countries started recruiting for the upcoming war. Romanticized nationalistic pride took over as the people joined the army to fight for their king and country. From Moscow to Paris, millions of young men were joining the army, and everyone expected the conflict to be brief and to end before Christmas. In Germany, people were enthusiastic about the war, thinking they would surely be the absolute winners. Their goal was to display Germany's military dominance over Europe. Even the Social Democrats abandoned their pacifist endeavors once they were persuaded that Russia was the aggressor. Oddly enough, the Jews who were openly oppressed not so long before during the reign of Wilhelm I and his grandson Wilhelm II, were enthusiastically joining the German army to help in the fight for the fatherland.

In the 1890s, Germany devised a secret strategy known as the Schlieffen Plan, which would allow for quick mobilization of the troops in the case of conflict on two fronts. The plan included a quick occupation of France by dispatching forces through neutral Belgium and Luxembourg. Paris would fall before Russia even started mobilizing its army (due to the lack of infrastructure throughout the vast Russian regions). After taking France, Germany would easily turn its attention towards the east and help Austria fight Russia. While Germany occupied France, Austria planned to invade Serbia and later confront Russia. The plan was detailed, and it also relied on Italian help. But Italy declared it would stay neutral during the war. Without Italy, Germany and Austria were surrounded by their enemies and were known as the Central Powers. They had the promise of the Turkish sultan that he would join their alliance, but they could not rely on his word. Nevertheless, Germany continued with its plans and mobilized over 1.5 million soldiers.

During their crossing of Belgium, the German army immediately encountered a problem. They didn't think Belgium would organize resistance, but their passage through the neutral country was halted for a time when Belgian resistance caused them significant losses. The Germans had violated Belgian neutrality guaranteed by the treaty of 1837, and Britain reacted by joining the war on the side of France and Russia in the alliance known as the Triple Entente. The British army hurried to France to help slow the German occupation. The French army was stationed near the German border, as it hoped it could be faster and invade Germany. However, the French now had to move their army south to Paris, and mobilization was very slow. The first conflict between France and Germany occurred in September at the Battle of Marne, where the French managed to halt the German advance. Unfortunately, they too suffered great losses, and the conflict bogged down to a stalemate. Pushed by their officers, the young soldiers of both sides lost their lives in a fruitless offensive on enemy positions. Suffering trench fires and brutal assaults, the western front yielded no results for over four years. Millions of lives were lost in the suicide mission to advance towards the enemy territory, but neither side could make a decisive breakthrough. The Schlieffen Plan failed, and Germany was forced to divide its army and fight on two fronts.

The Russians surprised everyone by proving that the bad infrastructure of their empire, with its lack of railroads, was not a problem when it came to the mobilization of their army. Russians invaded East Prussia quickly. But a pair of brilliant German generals, Paul von Hindenburg and Erich Ludendorff, smashed their further advance. Back in Germany, they were celebrated as national heroes, and their victory over Russia helped lift the nationalistic spirit of the people even more. New recruits were pouring into the army and, very quickly, Germany was ready to invade Russia's Polish territories. But the campaigns in the east, although very successful, were short-lived, and Germany soon had to assume a defensive stance once again.

Austria managed to take Belgrade (the capital of Serbia) early during the conflict, but it also suffered great casualties. Because of this, Serbs managed to expel the Austrians in early 1915, and the Habsburg forces spent the rest of the year trying to invade Italy. To quickly deal with Serbia, Germany and Austria persuaded Bulgaria to join the war and invade Serbian territories. Pressured from the east by Bulgaria and from the west by Austria-Hungary, the Serbian army was crushed and forced to retreat through Albania. Through the snowy mountain ranges of Albania, the Serbian army suffered frost, hunger, and disease. More than 240,000 soldiers died in this endeavor, promptly named the "Albanian Golgotha" (the place where Jesus was crucified). Germany considered this a victory and, on November 29, 1915, issued a proclamation stating that the Serbian army was destroyed and that the Balkan front was closed. The Russian tsar had to intervene and threatened he would pull his army out of the war if allies France, Britain, and Italy didn't rush to rescue the Serbian army from Albania. The French president promised their transport ships would halt all transportations of goods and military equipment until the remnants of the Serbian army were delivered to safety. Around 5,000 soldiers died during the transportation, and they were buried at sea, near the small island of Vido (part of Greece). In their honor, Greek fishermen refused to catch fish in the area for the next fifty years.

The horrors of modern warfare took victims on all fronts. The similar destiny of suffering soldiers occurred throughout the continent. The industrial age had produced modern guns and rifles, and war became even more brutal, with millions of victims on both sides. The main tactic of World War I was to break the enemy's resolve through mass infantry attacks on their bases and trenches. The soldiers of both sides were constantly exposed to machine-gun fire and artillery bombardment, but the bloodiest battles of this conflict were waged in France. Verdun and the Somme were the scenes of the bloodiest carnage in Europe in 1916. The stalemate at Somme lasted for years, and more than a million soldiers lost their lives in futile attempts to overpower their opposers. Desperate to break the stalemate, Germans unleashed the horrors of chemical warfare, using poisonous mustard gas against French soldiers and leaving them to die in agony. The British army introduced innovative primitive tanks designed to crush enemy troops. Even with the use of such modern weaponry and chemicals, after three years of constant fighting, the western front barely managed to move ten miles (16 km).

Wilhelm II lost his faith in German military power as victory slipped out of his hands. But aside from its inability to move the western front forward, Germany also replaced its civilian leadership for a military government. Due to the prolonged war, the country's economy suffered, and all that kept the people from revolting against their government were the victories on the eastern front. Russians were pushed to a retreat, and in Moscow, both soldiers and workers rioted. The imperialistic government was toppled, and Tzar Nicholas II was forced to abdicate. In November 1917, the Bolsheviks took over Russia, and Germany helped install Communist leader Vladimir Lenin (1870–1924) in Russia. In turn, Lenin sued for peace with Germany, taking Russia out of the war. By the Treaty of Brest-Litovsk signed between Germany and Russia, Germany gained control over the Polish territories as well as the Baltic States, Finland, and Ukraine. The Allies saw through the punitive nature of this treaty and used it as propaganda to deal harshly with the Germans during the rest of the war. Back home, German radical Socialists realized the imperialistic intentions behind Germany's involvement in the war and started their own propaganda, which helped turn the workers against the war. Germany was on the verge of failing in its war efforts. However, the government managed to deal with the workers' strikes and continue the war.

By 1918, the United States joined the war and sent troops to the western front to help relieve the French and British army. As the Germans could no longer bear the stalemate at Somme, they planned a final, massive assault along the whole western front, which ranged from Belgium to northeastern France, Switzerland, and the German territories in the northwest. In March, the Germans managed to push the front seventy-five miles from Paris and started shelling the French capital. In Berlin, celebrations had already started, as everyone believed victory was near. But the Allies refused to surrender, and they managed to hold the position for months. German soldiers were already at the end of their strength by July when the Allies managed to push them back to their previous trench position on the Belgian border. Germans sacrificed more than 250,000 soldiers during this last offensive, and they gained nothing. This costly defeat was a final straw for the civilians of Germany. Soon, anti-war demonstrations swept the whole country as people wondered why they had allowed more than six million German soldiers to die.

At the same time, Austria, Turkey, and Bulgaria started losing the war on the eastern front. Bulgaria and Turkey were the first to drop out of the war in early 1918, and Austria-Hungary sued for peace on November 3, 1918. The nationalist uprisings throughout the Habsburg Empire shook Austria, and it could no longer support the war. Germany suddenly found itself completely alone against the Allied powers, and it anxiously accepted defeat. It was the new liberal chancellor from Baden, Prince Maximilian (1867–1929), who carried the full authority to negotiate peace. He approached the Americans, first offering to accept their proposal of a post-war settlement based on national self-determination. But American President Woodrow Wilson refused to negotiate with Germany due to its imperialistic nature and intentions during the war. The situation back in Germany reached dangerous levels as the people continued to protest the war. Even the navy mutinied and caused such chaos in Germany that the Kaiser's advisors started pressing Wilhelm II to abdicate. Wilhelm didn't want to part with the crown, so he offered to abandon his imperial titles and remain king of Prussia. But it was too late for compromises. On November 9, 1918, Prince Maximilian of Baden proclaimed to the public that Emperor Wilhelm II had abdicated. Germany fragmented into a series of ethnic enclaves, and all the ex-emperor could do was sit back and watch his empire crumble.

Fearing that the Communists would take control over Germany after the emperor stepped down, a Socialist politician, Philipp Scheidemann, declared the rise of the German Republic. He had no authority to act, and the radical leaders responded by announcing the start of a Communist regime. Prince Maximilian resigned as chancellor out of the fear of the approaching Communist revolution, and power was handed to Socialist leader Friedrich Ebert. On November 10, Ebert managed to establish a provisional government comprised of Social Democratic Party members. Their first task was to replace the old imperial constitution with a new one more suitable for the German Republic. The Republic was organized with an elected president and a chancellor appointed by the Reichtag. But before any of this could be done, the provisional government had to officially end the war. On the 11th hour, of the 11th day, of the 11th month, Germany finally accepted defeat and capitulated to the Triple Entente. Almost ten million lives lost later, World War I ended.

The Weimar Republic

At the end of World War I, the Treaty of Versailles was signed, by which Germany lost many of its territories gained before and during the war. Alsace-Lorraine France had to be returned to France, and the territories gained with the Treaty of Brest-Litovsk were lost. The treaty also disarmed Germany, obliging it to have an army limited to only 100,000 men and no fleet, submarines, or airplanes. Germans also had to accept responsibility for the whole war and pay an indemnity of more than thirty-two billion US dollars. French troops occupied the Rhineland until the full amount of money was paid. The Treaty of Versailles left the citizens of Germany in shock. They had a hard time accepting responsibility for the war since they had no part in the Austrian provocations of Serbia. Furthermore, German propaganda insisted that Germany didn't lose the war since its territories were never occupied. Germans held to the fact that their forces retreated from the war in goodwill, and they felt that they were harshly punished without reason. The people felt that the provisional government had betrayed them by allowing such a draconic punishment to happen. But the truth was that the German provisional government had no other choice but to agree to the terms of the victorious Allied Powers.

The situation in Germany only escalated. Inspired by the Russian Bolsheviks, a Communist group known as the Spartacists arose. Their leaders, Rosa Luxemburg and Karl Liebknecht, organized a massive rebellion in Berlin. Still, the post-war elections continued, and the new government emerged while the army was dealing with the rebellion in Berlin. Even though Rosa Luxemburg and Karl Liebknecht were killed during the brutal crackdown of the uprising, the Communists continued their violent revolution. The government, mostly made up out of SDP members but also consisting of Radical Socialists and Catholic Centre, had to retreat to Weimar so it could work on the constitution. The violence on the streets of Berlin continued, and it started spreading to other cities in Germany. But the country elected a new president, SDP statesman Friedrich Ebert. He ratified the new constitution, which was a remarkably progressive document guaranteeing democratic rights and participation for all citizens. The German president would serve for seven years, while the members of the National Assembly (Reichstag) served for four years. The national elections would determine how many seats each political party would occupy during the four-year mandates. The president's duty was to elect a chancellor who would form a cabinet and, with its help, govern the state. Even though the government formed in this way was liberal and a true representative of the republic and its people, many resented it for accepting the terms of the Treaty of Versailles. They also saw the problem in Article 48 of the new constitution, which gave the president the right to dismiss the constitution and the Reichstag in times of crisis. This would allow the president to wield absolutist power in the case of a new war, something the German populace dreaded.

From the beginning, the Weimar Republic was unstable and suffered the attacks of radical political groups. In 1920, these attacks turned into an uprising when Wolfgang Kapp, an ardent nationalist, led Freikorps (a volunteer military unit) soldiers to occupy Berlin and overthrow the government. But his attempt was unsuccessful, mainly because he had no support from the people. In Bavaria, right-wing extremists were more successful. Munich was turned into the main hub for radical nationalists. Communists were on the move, too. In Ruhr, they started a workers' uprising that required the intervention of militia. Soon, the French got involved, and to pacify the Ruhr region, they occupied it in 1923. But the result was the opposite of what they hoped to achieve. The occupation only inflamed radical nationalism, and although passive, resistance continued. All these uprisings and attempts to overthrow the government didn't bring anything good to Germany. Its economic recovery after the war was slowed down by the political instability within the country. The German national currency became nearly worthless, and people found themselves unable to afford a loaf of bread. The Weimar government printed new bills, trying to keep pace with inflation, but this only made things worse. It was this economic crisis that sparked further political unrest, and another failed coup occurred in 1923 at the Munich Beer Hall. However, this putsch was led by an ambitious military veteran and politician, Adolf Hitler.

The Weimar government managed to prevent the total collapse of the German economy by issuing a new currency, and the economy slowly recovered. With a better standard of living, the violent uprisings started calming down. But the improvement of the situation in Germany was only an illusion. The state entered a new phase: the calm before the storm. In the second half of the 1920s, Germany saw economic, cultural, and political renewal, and its post-war diplomatic isolation ended. Relations with Britain, France, and the United States were repaired, and the Allied forces even decided to soften the sanctions against Germany. The Dawes Plan, signed in 1924, convinced Britain and France to lower the war reparations Germany still owed. By 1926, foreign relations were so good that Germany was even invited to join the League of Nations. Berlin's abundant nightlife and cultural ascent gave the impression of a better life—but the storm clouds were gathering above Germany once again. Socialist statesmen Ebert died in 1925, and a new president was elected, the aging war hero Paul von Hindenburg. The new president still held a grudge over the humiliating Treaty of Versailles, and he made a deal with the Soviet Union in 1926 by which the German army was permitted to train in Soviet territory. This way, the German military defied the post-war limitation to maintain a small army. Behind the back of the Allied forces, Germany was preparing for a new war.

In 1929, the world was shaken by another economic crisis known to history as the Great Depression. The US stock market crashed, and the loans it was giving to Germany had to cease. Without these loans, Germany's economy faltered, as it was once again drowning in the debts of the war indemnity. The very next year, the consequences of the Great Depression were very severe in Germany. Businesses were shut down, factories had to stop producing, and the unemployment rates skyrocketed. German society was in the clutches of fear and desperation, while its government proved unable to fight the new crisis. The spreading anxiety was a perfect breeding ground for the rise of radical nationalism, and in the new elections held in 1930, the radical political parties won. The SDP managed to hold the most chairs in the National Assembly (24%), but the National Socialist Party, better known as the Nazi Party, won an unbelievable 18% of the chairs. The radical Communists also had a very high number, at 13%. The Reichstag was often in conflict as the dramatically different political parties argued about new legislation. But the fighting wasn't kept within the Reichstag, soon pouring onto the streets of Berlin and other major cities of Germany. Fights between the Nazis and the Communists, who were unable to maintain a democratic parliament, resulted in bloodshed in the streets. The situation quickly escalated, and President Hindenburg felt forced to invoke Article 48 of the constitution, which granted him the power to make all the decisions in the case of a state emergency. The Weimar Republic was destroyed by the economic crisis and by the radical political parties which won the elections.

Chapter 11 – World War II

Warsaw, the capital of Poland, in ruins
https://commons.wikimedia.org/wiki/File:Warsaw_Old_Town_1945.jpg

Hitler's Rise and Nazism in Germany

Adolf Hitler at a political rally in 1933

In 1932, Adolf Hitler almost won the new presidential elections but
was defeated by the old Hindenburg, who somehow managed to get
53% of the votes. Adolf Hitler was an obscure Austrian who
migrated to Bavaria right before World War I. He enlisted in the
German army, where he found a sense of belonging after his failed
career as an artist. Even after the war, he continued working for the
German army as a spy, monitoring the radical political parties
emerging in Germany after the war. He also held resentment for the
Treaty of Versailles and Germany's loss of the war. But instead of
accepting defeat, he found scapegoats to blame: the Socialists and
the Jews. Even though Jews massively joined the German army
during the war, Hitler convinced the people that Jews were nothing

more than foreign traitors who backstabbed Germany, sabotaging its war efforts. To bolster his political career, Hitler joined the German Workers' Party in 1919 and quickly climbed to leadership of the organization. Soon he changed the name of the party to the National Socialist German Workers' Party (NSDAP), shortened to the Nazi Party. He often spoke against the Weimar Republic, and his passion quickly attracted people to him. During the Beer Hall Putsch in Munich (1923), he was jailed for nine months. He took that time to write his manifesto, known as *Mein Kampf.* In it, he carefully chronicled his twisted delusions about the superiority of the German race and described how Jews and previous Socialist Party stood in the way of German greatness. By 1932, Hitler's Nazi Party became a massive political force that continued to grow, fueled by people's resentment towards the Treaty of Versailles and the inability of the current government to deal with the economic crisis of the Great Depression.

In the Reichstag elections of 1932, the Nazi party won 38% of the votes, surpassing the previously popular SDP, which won only 21%. The Communist Party was far behind, with only 14% of the votes. Despite the obvious win, President Hindenburg refused to make Adolf Hitler his chancellor. Instead, he chose military officer Franz von Papen, who soon proved to be unpopular among the delegates of the Reichstag and the people. The elections had to be repeated, and the Nazis' growing popularity won them over 200 seats in the National Assembly. Hitler's growing popularity was a concern, but Hindenburg saw replacing von Papen as an opportunity to get back on Germany's political scene. He formed a coalition between the German National People's Party (DNVP) and the Nazis. When von Papen promised Hindenburg he could control the Nazis, the president finally agreed to make Hitler his chancellor. On January 30, 1933, Adolf Hitler officially became Germany's chancellor, with von Papen as his vice-chancellor. Only a year later, Hitler assumed the title "führer" (leader), ending the Weimar democracy.

Since 1926, the Nazi Party had held annual meetings in Nuremberg, providing Hitler with a great opportunity to spread his propaganda. In 1934, the meeting gathered more than one million Germans, and the famous young filmmaker and photographer, Leni Riefenstahl, was tasked with bringing Hitler's vision of Aryan superiority to life. Her movie, the *Triumph of the Will,* was proclaimed one of the most successful and dangerous propaganda movies in the world. The film shows Hitler delivering one of his maniacal speeches to the assembled masses. Through careful choreography of the masses and innovative shots, Leni delivered a message of German purity to those who couldn't attend the meeting in person. But what she failed to convey through her movie was the Nazis' real intention—to purify Germany of non-Aryan elements through war and extermination. For Hitler, the biggest danger to national unity and greatness were the Jews, Communists, and both physically and mentally impaired people. Only with these dangers out of sight could Germany conquer other nations and climb to sit on top of the world's order.

Hitler's speeches were filled with crude and violent rhetoric. This appealed to a population that already resented the Jews and feared the Communists. No matter what classes they came from, supporters flocked around their new führer. Traumatized by the Great Depression, middle-class citizens and workers of Germany, as well as old war veterans and young members of the Freikorps, all supported the Nazis and their charismatic leader. Students and intellectuals weren't spared—the mass media used to spread Nazi propaganda appealed to them, too. Attracted by the technology the party used, as well as by its efficiency and racial pseudoscience, universities succumbed to Hitler's propaganda.

In 1933, Hitler also invoked Article 48 of the Weimar Republic constitution and took emergency power into his hands. He used it to outlaw the SDP and thus eliminate the only remaining opposition to his political ideals. Thousands of leftists were arrested, but he did not stop there. He also persecuted the right-wing politicians who dared to challenge him. By summer, the Nazi Party was the only political entity within Germany. To completely unify the state under his ideology, Hitler gradually outlawed independent trade unions as well as the country's state governments. In 1933, the Jews of Germany started feeling the first signs of oppression caused by the rabid anti-Semitism of the Nazis. Jewish civil servants, teachers, and jurists were the first to be removed from their posts. In the end, Hitler took control of all German media, and opposition newspapers and radio stations were banned. He chose a propaganda minister, Joseph Goebbels, whose task was to not only convey the Nazi ideology to the masses but also control all the media people were consuming.

June 30, 1934, is remembered as the "Night of the Long Knives," when, under the command of Heinrich Himmler, Nazis murdered their own party members who were considered unfit. Among them were members of the Sturmabteilung (Storm Detachment), the most radical Nazi paramilitary wing. Their leader, Ernst Röhm, died that night, too. Hitler justified this purge of the party by claiming their radicalism could eventually lead to separation. Only through murder could he consolidate his dominion over the whole Nazi Party. The publicity approved of Hitler's authority, and as soon as President Hindenburg died on August 2, 1934, Hitler proclaimed himself führer, the leader of Germany, putting an end to any possible individual claims on leadership.

Once Hitler consolidated his power, he started working to repair the German economy and army. He established his inner circle, made of Minister of Propaganda Goebbels, Reichsführer Himmler, and the military leader Hermann Göring, and together they worked to make Germany a powerhouse of Europe. Göring used the industrial factories that had succumbed to the Great Depression to start military production. Consequently, Germany's unemployment rates decreased, while its manufacturing production increased. The workers and the industrialists were so delighted with the economic rise of Germany that they were ready to forgive their lack of democratic freedoms. However, even though Hitler enjoyed widespread support, he also had to rely on terror and violence. As early as 1933, he formed a secret police force, the Gestapo, and outlined plans for a system of concentration camps where Jews and political and criminal prisoners labored and died in horrible conditions. In 1935, the appearance of the Nuremberg Laws excluded Jews from German citizenship. This set of laws strictly defined how to classify Jews and non-Aryans and forbade marriage and intercourse between Jews and Germans. Only those who were of pure German blood and their relatives were eligible for Reich citizenship. The rest had no rights and were considered only to be the Reich's subjects. Jews were strictly forbidden from employing German females younger than forty-five to prevent the accidental mix of blood. By 1938, cities across Germany constructed ghettos, where the Jews were to live in confinement.

The night of November 9, 1938, is remembered as the Kristallnacht (the Night of the Broken Glass), when Goebbels' anti-Semitic propaganda fueled the German population into a violent rage. Thousands of Jewish homes, businesses, and temples were destroyed, and countless Jews were beaten, killed, or taken to the concentration camps. To avoid further oppression, more than half of Germany's Jews escaped the country. Those who stayed did so willingly to take care of aging family members or protect family businesses built over the generations. Many even stayed in hopes that the madness would soon pass because they believed it couldn't last for long. While his accomplices continued anti-Semitic pogroms across the country, Hitler focused on rebuilding the army with which he would conquer Europe and provide living space for the superior Aryans. His first move was to withdraw Germany from the League of Nations and take back the industrial heartland of Germany, the Saarland, which had been under French occupation since the end of the war. In 1935, the League of Nations organized a plebiscite in Saarland, and 90% of its citizens chose to join

Germany rather than stay under French rule. Inspired by this non-aggressive victory, Hitler declared he was pulling Germany out of the restrictions imposed by the Treaty of Versailles and that he was building the army. The European powers were alarmed, and Britain, France, and Italy met to discuss how they would react. But, since they could not come up with a unanimous resolution, Hitler continued with his activities unopposed.

In 1936, the Spanish Civil War raged, and Hitler took the opportunity of Europe in dismay to make another threat. He declared that Germany would no longer respect the territorial boundaries imposed on her after World War I and that it would seek to expand towards the west. This was a direct threat to France, but Britain was unwilling to risk the war and voted against new sanctions on Germany during the meeting of the League of Nations. This divide between the European allies was proof enough for Hitler that he had no strong opposition. He moved his troops to the Rhineland, violating the Treaty of Versailles. However, France and its allies decided not to respond, and the opportunity to deal with the Nazis early on was lost. Through its inaction, Europe allowed Hitler to rejuvenate the German military and sway the whole of Germany into his megalomania.

Hitler planned for war, and to successfully lead one, he needed allies. First, in July of 1936, he turned to his native Austria, which he already planned to absorb into Nazi Germany. By October, he signed an agreement with Italy's fascist leader, Benito Mussolini. He also sent troops to Spain to help their fascist leader, General Franco, to overthrow the republican government. Japan joined last, at the end of 1936, and concluded the formation of the aggressive coalition known as the Axis Powers. To stop the outbreak of war, European powers started caving to Hitler's demands in hopes of appeasing him. First in the series of demands was to bring all the Germans living in the neighboring countries under the rule of the Third Reich. Nazi leaders called their country the "Third Reich," as it followed the Second (the German Empire ruled by Wilhelm I and Wilhelm II). The First Reich was considered to be the Holy Roman Empire started by Emperor Otto in 962.

To unify Austria and Germany, Hitler moved his troops on March 9, 1938, and they entered Vienna. Hitler followed four days later and was cheered by the pro-Nazi masses, which called for Austria's absorption into the Third Reich. All the European powers could do while watching Hitler's rise to power was complain, and they remained inactive even when Austria was taken. Hitler's next target was the multiethnic republic of Czechoslovakia. There, Hitler became a hero and representative of ethnic Germans living within the republic's Sudetenland, an industrial region on the border with Germany. Supported by their native country, the Germans of Sudetenland started holding demonstrations, demanding the autonomy of the region. To support the cause in Czechoslovakia, German troops started gathering on the border. Britain tried to resolve the situation and sent Prime Minister Neville Chamberlain to talk some sense into the German leader. But Hitler threatened open warfare over Sudetenland, and the Europeans backed down again. France and Britain allowed Hitler to annex this region, but they promised to defend the rest of Czechoslovakia if the need arose. Seeing the perfect opportunity to start the war he desperately wanted, Hitler claimed all of Czechoslovakia, but, in the end, agreed to negotiate. On September 29, 1938, he met with the leaders of Britain, France, and Italy, and they settled on the Munich Agreement, by which all regions of Czechoslovakia inhabited by Germans would vote whether they wanted to join the Third Reich. What was left of the republic would be protected by Britain and France. While the British celebrated avoiding war, Hitler moved his troops through Czechoslovakia. In March of 1939, the German army overran the republic, and Hitler led his victorious soldiers through Prague. Britain and France did nothing to stop him, even though they promised the safeguard of Czechoslovakia.

Britain and France made similar promises of safeguard to Poland in case of German aggression, but Czechoslovakia proved to Hitler that they wouldn't do anything. By April of 1939, he planned a full-scale invasion of Poland and started negotiating with Soviet leader Joseph Stalin. In August of 1939, they made a non-aggression pact, which they used to peacefully divide Poland between themselves. In the meantime, the Nazi Party financed the Germans of Danzig (Gdansk in modern-day Poland) to demand autonomy and create a pretext for invasion. Confident that the Soviet Union wouldn't meddle, Hitler started the invasion of Poland on September 1, 1939. However, he was wrong about France and Britain, as they declared war on Germany only two days later. World War II had started.

The Course of the War

London after the Blitz
https://commons.wikimedia.org/wiki/File:View_from_St_Paul%27s_Cathedral_after_the_Blitz.jpg

Germany started the war with new tactics, which involved an easily-movable force consisting of speedy tanks that were supported by air attacks. The goal was a quick victory and conquest of territories before the enemy realized what had hit them. The tactic was conveniently named blitzkrieg, the "lightning war." Although the blitzkrieg strategy was first used in 1936 during the Spanish Civil War, now Hitler was attacking Poland. The mechanized infantry and tank divisions attacked violently and quickly, while dedicated special units interrupted Polish communication and supply lines, creating confusion and fear. Poland didn't even have time to mobilize its army before the blitzkrieg was over. But German victory wasn't only due to these new, innovative tactics. Hitler's earlier deal with Stalin put Poland between two enemies. While more than two million German troops invaded from the west and raced towards Warsaw, the Russian army attacked from the east. The Poles weren't prepared for two fronts, and there was nothing they could do to stop the invasions. Warsaw fell on September 27, 1939, and Poland was divided between the Germans and the Russian dictator.

Blitzkrieg surprised not only Poland but also the British and the French. Even though the two powers promised they would safeguard this country, they were unable to mobilize in time to mount a defense. They could only stand idly by and watch while Poland was being divided between the Nazis and the Soviets. Seeing how slow European powers were to react, Hitler set off to execute his big plan, "The Final Solution," with which he would exterminate all Jews. Even though the realization of the plan started in Europe, it was by no means constricted to this continent alone. Nazis dared to dream about world conquest and the spread of the Aryan race over all continents. Poland was just a starting point. The Jews were forced to wear a yellow Star of David so they could be easily recognized. Soon, their businesses and all their possessions were confiscated, and they were confined in the ghettos. Once in the ghettos, the Polish population of Jews started succumbing to hunger and disease. Over three million Jews were registered in Poland, and that number halved before the western Allies could react.

Hitler's move towards Poland gave Russia an excuse to invade the Baltic states of Latvia, Lithuania, and Estonia. The Soviets also had their eye on Finland, but they found this country to be much more resilient. The Germans conquered Denmark and Norway in March of 1940, while Britain and France still gathered their army. After their swift victories, the Germans installed puppet governments in the conquered areas, led by native Nazi sympathizers. In the spring of 1940, the Netherlands, Belgium, and Luxembourg were also conquered in preparation for the invasion of France. Once more, Hitler employed blitzkrieg tactics, and the Germans moved towards Paris with remarkable speed. There was no one to stop them. The British tried to help, sending their forces across the North Sea, but heavy German airplane bombardment had them stranded on the beach at Dunkirk, unable to move forward. The remaining British vessels tried to save their soldiers, and even local fishermen and pleasure yacht captains joined the rescue operation. In late May of 1940, more than 300,000 British and French soldiers managed to escape to England. But tens of thousands of them were killed during the German blitzkrieg. France was defeated, and it officially surrendered on June 22nd. Southern France was turned over to a puppet government under the leadership of collaborator Henri Philippe Pétain. In history, it remains known as Vichy France, the name of the resort town where the new government was headquartered.

It took Hitler only two weeks to conquer France, and his next goal was England. But the major challenge he faced was defeating the Royal Air Force that guarded the sky over the English Channel. The German Luftwaffe (Air Force) was commanded by Hitler's personal friend, Hermann Göring. The Battle of Britain soon began (July 10–October 31, 1940), and it proved to be one of the turning points of World War II. British and German bomber fleets were ruthless, and civilians also suffered from their attacks. Bombers fought not only each other but also the transportation network and some of the major industrial cities. London was bombed regularly. To save their capital, the British came up with the idea of turning off all lights during the night so the enemy pilots wouldn't be able to see the city and target it. The German cities weren't so lucky, and some of them were destroyed. Dresden, for example, was razed to the ground for being a major industrial and communication center. But this city was even more than that. It was a military strongpoint, a city designated to be a defense against a possible Soviet invasion. The Royal Air Force and the United States Army ruthlessly bombed the city for what it represented. However, most of the casualties, which numbered between 18,000 and 25,000, were women and children. For this reason, the bombing of Dresden is one of the most controversial Alliance actions of World War II.

Germany was never able to defeat the Royal Air Force, and by the early summer of 1941, Hitler abandoned his plans to conquer Britain. Instead, he turned against his former ally, Stalin. The relationship between two dictators had cooled off a year earlier when both Hitler and Stalin laid claim to the oil fields of Ploesti, in modern Romania. While the Germans warred against Britain, the Soviets annexed the Baltic states and took Basarabia, which was previously under Romanian control. Russians continued to put pressure on Romania, which decided to side with Germany and join the secret plan of invading Russia. For Hitler, Russia wasn't the enemy just because it claimed the oil. It was a matter of racial supremacy, as well. Like Jews, Slavs were a lesser race in Hitler's eyes, and their territory needed to be populated with the superior Aryan race. By 1941, Germany had conquered Yugoslavia as well as Hungary and Greece, making them a part of the Axis Powers. Hitler had his troops stations in the Balkans, where they prepared for the invasion of the Union of Soviet Socialist Republics (USSR). He made a deal with neutral Sweden and Finland to allow safe passage for the troops coming from Norway. Everything was set, and on June 22, 1941, under the code name Operation Barbarossa, the invasion of Russia began.

Over three million German troops crossed the Russian border from three different points: Finland, Poland, and Romania. Repeating the blitzkrieg tactics they had used to occupied France, Germany drove deep into the Russian territory. By December 21nd, the Red Army was almost defeated as Hitler's troops moved towards Moscow. Hitler's army had reached a position only fifteen miles outside the USSR capital when the bitter Russian winter halted their advance. Badly equipped, German troops froze in the field, dying of hunger and frost while the Red Army regrouped for a counterattack. Accustomed to harsh conditions, the Russian army had the advantage and managed to eventually drive the Germans out of the country. The Russian front was the bloodiest point of World War II. The atrocities committed in the Soviet Union are some of the harshest actions against humanity that history ever saw. Aside from killing off a million Russian Jews, Germans killed 3.3 million Red Army soldiers and an uncountable number of civilians. The methods used to deal with the Slavs varied from gassing to mass shootings and planned starvation. Hitler's goal was to confiscate food from people and redirect it to Germany while the Russian soldiers and civilians starved to death. The estimated Soviet death count during World War II is over twenty-six million, of which eleven million were soldiers. This number represents 95% of the war casualties between the three major Alliance forces: Britain, Russia, and the United States of America. The bloodiest battle of World War II, the Battle of Stalingrad (August 23, 1942–February 2, 1943) completely turned the tide of war. The losses Germany suffered during the five months of constant battle in front of this city were never again recouped. Even though Hitler redirected soldiers from the western front to the east, they were unable to achieve any more major victories on Russian soil. The eastern front was at a stalemate.

In the west, Germany still held sway over Europe. Japan forced the United States to join the war by bombing Pearl Harbor on December 7, 1941. The United States retaliated in the Battle of Midway (June 1942) by bombing the Japanese fleet, making it useless for the rest of the war. In October of 1942, the British and the Americans combined their forces to attack the Germans and Italians stationed in North Africa. Their success marked a change in the course of the war, but the war was far from over—the nightmare has only just begun. When Anglo-American forces landed on Sicily in June of 1943, the German alliance with Italy crumbled. Italians were forced to retreat from war while the Allied forces marched on Rome. A year later, the Americans entered Rome and Italy and joined the Allies against Nazi Germany. After a few days, the invasion of Normandy, known as D-day, took place.

On Tuesday, June 6, 1944, the massive force of Allied soldiers landed on the beaches of Normandy, in northern France. Under the codename Operation Neptune, the Allied forces disembarked the overseas carriers while the air force offered them protection. From the beaches of Normandy, they advanced to break the German garrisons and establish the Allies' foothold in France. At this point, the liberation of France (and later the rest of Europe) began. Allied forces were fighting their way forward while under the constant attack of the Germans, who defended their position in northern France. It took several months for the British and American soldiers to conquer some of the strategic points along the Normandy coast, but the efforts to bring warfare to Europe's mainland were successful. Gradually, the German frontier was pushed back, and the Nazi soldiers were forced to go on the defensive. Both eastern and western fronts saw a major change. By 1944, Germany felt its shortage of men, and those who survived fought a losing battle. The beginning of 1945 saw the Red Army of the Soviet Union ready to invade the German territories from the east, while the rest of the Allied forces would push from the west. But Hitler wouldn't give up. He still thought he could turn the tides of the war, but his big final plan never saw the light of day. In February of 1945, the Russians were nearing Berlin, while the Americans and the British were just crossing the Rhine. On April 30, 1945, finally realizing that Germany was helpless, Adolf Hitler committed suicide with his wife, Eva Braun. Two days later, Russians overran Berlin, and German forces everywhere started surrendering.

The official fall of Germany occurred on May 7, 1945. Admiral Karl Dönitz, who took control over Germany after Hitler, declared Germany's full surrender to the Supreme Commander of the Allied Expeditionary Force, General Dwight Eisenhower, who would later become the president of the United States. World War II—the result of one person's megalomania and Europe's unresolved problem after World War I—officially ended, leaving Europe in ruins. Germany was defeated and its people left in disgrace to further suffer foreign rule. The Soviets occupied eastern parts of Germany, and as if to punish the Germans for daring to invade mother Russia, they raped, pillaged, and murdered civilians. After the initial shock of losing the war, the people of Germany had to face the atrocities they had committed while under the spell of Hitler's propaganda. They had to confront the rest of the world, which blamed them for the deaths of millions of Jews and an uncountable number of soldiers and civilians.

The Holocaust

Map of Europe showing the location of all major concentration camps, massacres, and deportation routes

While the Germans fought the Red Army in the invasion of Russia, Hitler doubled his efforts to eradicate the Jews of Europe. He set up a special paramilitary organization known as the Einsatzgruppen to round up the Communists, the Gypsies, and the Jews for mass executions. These death squads of Einsatzgruppen were commanded by Heinrich Himmler and his Schutzstaffel, the Protection Squadron commonly known as the SS. The members of the SS were chosen for their racial purity and their devotion to Nazi ideology. They alone were responsible for the death of hundreds of thousands of people. But their methods were ineffective, and in January of 1942, the commanding SS officers gathered in Berlin to come up with the "Final Solution of the Jewish Question."

Himmler, who deeply believed in the Nazi ideology of racial purity, believed that the mass shootings were damaging the mental health of the SS soldiers. Besides that, they were inefficient when applied to large-scale mass extermination. Together with Hitler and another SS officer, Reinhard Heydrich, Himmler drafted concentration and work camps and planned their expansion with the addition of gas chambers in which people would be killed by poisonous gas. These camps were first raised in the occupied territories of Poland, and with time, in other parts of Europe as well. Some of the most well-known concentration camps are still in Poland, including Auschwitz and Treblinka, and they serve as standing monuments, reminders of the Holocaust and human brutality.

The Nazis were often aided by frightened local people or collaborators when they rounded up Jews for transport to the death camps. They used all the modern industrial infrastructure to help them realize their extermination plans. Aryan ideology was so important to Nazis that they diverted some of the resources needed for war to fuel the trains that took Jews to concentration camps. By the end of World War II, around six million Jews had died in the Holocaust. But they weren't the only ones. Germans imprisoned and executed political and religious dissidents, Soviet prisoners of war, the Gypsies, and all the people Nazis considered degenerate (racially impure, homosexuals, mentally and physically disabled, etc.).

When it was evident that Germany was losing the war, the mass extermination didn't stop. 1944 was the year most people were killed in Auschwitz—over 500,000. Jews from Hungary were sent there to be immediately killed. By mid-1944, Europe had lost two-thirds of its Jewish population to the Nazi regime. Facing the Soviet invasion from the east, the Germans quickly dismantled their death camps, leaving no evidence of what was going on in them. The surviving inmates were pushed on a death march to the camps in the west, in Germany or Austria. Sick, exhausted, and starved, many people were unable to finish their journey. If they fell behind, the Germans would immediately kill them. But in the west, the same destiny awaited them—the gas chamber and the cremation furnace. At the end of the war, when the Allied forces marched into German territories, they were horrified by the scenes they found in the camps. The unburied bodies of starved inmates numbered into the thousands in a single pile. The Red Cross took care of most of the Holocaust survivors, but many of them were past salvation. Some of them died due to malnutrition and the sicknesses they were exposed to in the camps even after the liberation.

Chapter 12 – Modern Germany

After World War II was over, the Allied powers gathered at the Potsdam Conference, which lasted from July 17th until August 2, 1945. The main goal was to decide what to do with Germany, which had surrendered unconditionally. The Allies divided Germany into four administrative territories to be governed by Britain, the United States, France, and the Soviet Union. The three western zones occupied by the British, French, and the Americans cooperated very closely, but the eastern zone under the Soviets strove for separatism. A dangerous rift between the east and the west was created, and even the former capital of Germany felt this division. Berlin was divided among the Allies, even though it was positioned deep within the Soviet zone. However, the western powers had free access to their part of the city to supply people with everything they might need.

While the western powers worked to stabilize the economy of post-war Germany, Russia concentrated on tightening its grip on Eastern Europe. When the Allies issued a common currency for the entirety of Germany to improve the conditions within the country, Russia responded with anger.

Post-War Germany

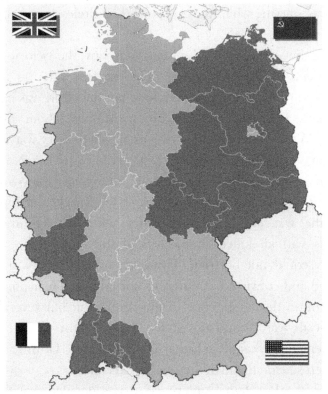

The occupation and division of Germany

WikiNight2, GFDL <http://www.gnu.org/copyleft/fdl.html>, via Wikimedia Commons
https://commons.wikimedia.org/wiki/File:Deutschland_Besatzungszonen_8_Jun_1947_-
_22_Apr_1949.svg

After the war, the German nation, as well as its country, was in ruins. Many Germans lost their homes in the ruthless bombing of major German cities at the end of the war. Millions of refugees of German ethnicities poured into the country once they lost their homes in the German-controlled territories of Czechoslovakia, Poland, the Baltic States, and other Balkan countries. They required homes, sustenance, and medical care. But they were not the only ones. More than a million ex-inmates from concentration camps had to be provided for by the Allies. Some were willing to leave Germany and settle in the United States or Britain, but many decided to stay and search for their lost family, homes, or possessions. The chaos of war brought hunger to Germany, and the nation was starving while the Allies worked tirelessly to rebuild the country.

Before they could start rebuilding Germany, the victorious Allies had to denazify the population. This started with the arrest of former Nazi officials and collaborators, but the effort was expanded to civilians, who were thoroughly questioned about their war activities. War crime tribunals were established to try war atrocities and other violations of human rights. Known as the Nuremberg Trials, they were conducted under the international laws of war to justly punish those who were responsible for Nazi leadership as well as for the war crimes. Adolf Hitler, Heinrich Himmler, and Goebbels had all killed themselves at the end of the war and obviously could not be tried. However, twenty-four Nazi officials were tried and convicted of different war crimes. Their punishment varied from a death sentence to imprisonment, but several of the high officials were found not guilty. Among those who received a death sentence was Reichsmarsall Hermann Göring, but he committed suicide the night before his execution.

During the Potsdam Conference, it was decided that Germany should pay war indemnities to the Allies worth $23 billion. However, since the country was in a post-war economic crisis, the Allies agreed that the payment could be made in industrial machinery and materials. Many factories were closed and dismantled, and Germany never fully paid the war reparation in money. But the Allies took Germany's scientists, intellectuals, and civilians and conscripted them into forced labor in France, Britain, the United States, Belgium, and in occupied Germany. But while western Allies worked on repairing Germany, the Soviet Union sought to make its eastern part into a Communist puppet state. They dismantled all of Eastern Germany's industries and sent them to Russia by railroad. The banks and remaining factories were nationalized, and soon the Soviets started confiscating agricultural land so it could be converted into communal production zones modeled after the Communist regime. German Communists were sent to the Soviet Union for training, and once they were back in their home country, they would be assigned administrative jobs. The first political parties to emerge in the east were the Soviet-sanctioned Communist Party and the Social Democratic Party. They were both up and running in 1945, but later that year, they merged to form a single party known as the Socialist Unity Party (SED).

Denazification efforts in eastern parts of Germany were extremely effective, as the Communists strived to create a Marxist-Leninist utopian state. Former Nazi officials were all executed, while the collaborators were sent to reeducation camps. After 1946, German youth were obliged to join the Free German Youth organization, in which they would be indoctrinated with Communist ideology. Women organized their Democratic Women's League to advocate equality and fight for women's rights in universities, workplaces, and government. The Soviet Union was rebuilding Germany in its image, but so were the rest of the Allies. In the west, a new democratic government was established with the purpose of building a capitalist enterprise in the occupied zones. The zone administered by the United States developed more quickly than any other. But the denazification wasn't as successful as in the east. Western Allies feared Communism would spread from the east and thus allowed some of the Nazi officials to remain in state administration. In West Germany, political parties also emerged, the first being the Christian Democratic Union (CDU). CDU was a conservative alliance of Catholics and Protestants who advocated for capitalism in Germany.

The western zones, which were administered by the United States, France, and Britain, unified under a single administration in the spring of 1949. But the Cold War was about to start, as the West and East couldn't agree on the transfer of war reparations between the zones. Open conflict never broke, but the ideological struggle between the Soviet Union and its Communist allies and the

United States and its western allies started. The rest of the 20th century would be dominated by this cold conflict fought with propaganda, espionage, and proxy wars in distant lands. It was British ex-Prime Minister Winston Churchill who came up with the term "the Iron Curtain" in 1946 to describe the dictatorship and Communist control which had descended upon Eastern Europe. Soon, the Iron Curtain became a reality as the east became separated from the democratic nations of the capitalist west.

By 1947, Europe was still feeling the effects of the war and struggled to revive its economy. The United States announced its plan (named the Marshall Plan) to give billions of dollars of aid to European countries to rebuild their economies and provide the United States with a market for its exports. Germany was one of the countries hit the hardest by the economic crisis, as its industry and railroad network was completely dismantled by the Allied forces. The people were malnourished and ill, their homes destroyed in the bombings during the last days of the war. The Soviet Union feared that its allied Communist states of Eastern Europe would desire the aid America was offering, so they forbade the states to take part in the Marshall Plan. But this only widened the gap between West and East. Once the US aid arrived in Western Europe in 1948, the economy was suddenly boosted. The result was not only the rejuvenation of the western European nations but also the creation of economic and military ties with the United States. Europe started integrating under one economic administration, and the first idea of the European Union was born during the Cold War. The areas of Germany administered by the Allies received more than one billion US dollars in aid, which only deepened the divide between western and eastern Germany. The fast development of western Germany angered the Soviets, and they retreated from the joint administration of Germany.

Provoked by the American Marshall Plan, the Soviets announced, in June 1948, that they would cut off all the railroads and roads leading from western to eastern parts of Germany. This meant that even those parts of Berlin which were under western administration would be cut off. The inhabitants of West Berlin were threatened with starvation, as the Allies wouldn't be able to supply them. The Soviets hoped that the western Allies would be forced to beg them to supply West Berlin, giving them de facto control over the entire city. Instead, they started the largest aerial relief operation, known as the Berlin Airlift. It lasted from June 1948 until May 1949, and the British, Americans, and French demonstrated not only their will and resolve to help Berlin but also their power and dominance over the Soviet Union. Around two million tons of supplies were delivered in what remains the biggest aerial relief operation in human history. Once the Soviets realized that the Allies had the resources and will to supply Berlin with necessities, they decided to lift the blockade. But the blockade itself wasn't about Germany. It represented the growing animosity between the East and the West, between Russia and the Allied forces.

Realizing the power of their alliance, the western powers continued to work together to create a new German state. They gathered representatives of all three western zones in Bonn on July 1, 1948, to draft a constitution for a united, federal state. Delegates from the German states created the constitution of West Germany, renaming it the Federal Republic of Germany (Bundesrepublik Deutschland, or BRD). The constitution guaranteed various civil rights, the establishment of a government, and a judiciary system. The new republic would have a president, a chancellor, and two legislatures bodies (the Bundestag and the Bundesrat) to govern the nation of West Germany. When the first Bundestag elections were held in August 1949, the CDU won a majority, with the Social Democratic Party (SDP) claiming only a handful of seats. Konrad Adenauer of the CDU was elected the first chancellor of Bundesrepublik, while Theodor Heuss of the Free Democrats was elected president. He was an ardent liberal, and although his position within the government was largely ceremonial, he worked hard to repair Germany's reputation on the international level.

In the east, Russians were busy creating their own Communist puppet state in Germany. The German Democratic Republic (GDR) was founded on October 7, 1949, in the zone administered by the Soviet Union. The GDR constitution was different than the BRD's, calling for the formation of a single legislative body, the Volkskammer, which would elect the members of the Council of State, an executive body. The GDR was never recognized by West Germany and its western allies, but the division of Germany was already set in stone. The border between the Federal Republic of Germany and the German Democratic Republic was a front line of the Cold War fought in Europe.

The Two Germanies

The western Allies ended their occupation of Germany in 1949, leaving it in the capable hands of its new chancellor, Konrad Adenauer. The new leader was quick to earn the trust of his people and his western allies. He served five terms (from 1949 until 1963) and brought progress, stability, and continuity to Germany. Slowly, through effort, Germany was leaving the chaos left by World War II. In the east, the GDR was under the leadership of able and determined statesmen, Wilhelm Pieck, who had fled to Moscow when the Nazis took over Germany and soon became Stalin's trusted associate. Elected by the Volkslammer, Pieck became the first president of the GDR in 1949. Together with Otto Grotewohl, first prime minister of GDR, Pieck started building a new Communist state in Europe in the image of the Soviet Union. After the death of Wilhelm Pieck in 1960, power was transferred to the leader of the dominant Socialist Unity Party, Walter Ulbricht. He constructed the central economy of East Germany, intending to rebuild and industrialize his country.

In response to the Marshall Plan, the Soviets formed the Council of Mutual Economic Assistance (COMECON), an organization that would help them plan the central economies of their Communist puppet states. Under its direction, the GDR issued a five-year plan that ambitiously called for the nationalization of all industry and agricultural land. But to meet the five-year quota, the plan focused heavily on pressuring the workers and bureaucrats spreading discontent. In 1953, the government demanded an increase in the production quota, and the workers had no other choice but to take to the streets in protest. Strikes and mass demonstrations took over the cities as the people demanded changes. The government responded with violence, and backed by the Soviet tanks and army, the security forces of GDR quelled the demonstrations. Hundreds of German workers were killed before the end of the uprising. The remaining workers were forced back into the factories without even the promise of better conditions in the future. Even though the five-year-plan failed, Ulbricht's government issued another even more ambitious plan in 1956. The quotas were again increased dramatically, but this time through the modernization of industry and collectivization of agriculture. But the GDR was incapable of achieving the rapid economic recovery of West Germany. East Germany lagged heavily behind the West, but in the Soviet sphere of influence, it became the economic leader capable of exporting produced goods into the rest of Eastern Europe.

The 1950s proved to be much more gentle in Western Germany, where the economy recovered with astonishing speed thanks to capable leadership and the Marshall Plan. In Germany, this period is remembered as the "economic miracle," as the government managed to integrate the millions of war refugees into the capitalist ideology of the West. The government of West Germany let the economy follow the rules of the free market, with only nominal direction and regulation. However, the consequences of the war were still visible among the civilians of Germany, and to provide social security for its people, West Germany came up with an extensive social welfare system. During the 1950s, Germany transformed from a war-torn and devastated country to a leading economic power, not only in Europe but also in the world.

The economy wasn't the only aspect in which West Germany thrived. Its chancellor and president worked tirelessly to improve the reputation of Germany, destroyed in World War II. To continue forward, Germany had to make amends with the survivors of the Nazi regime, and the government in Bonn agreed to pay billions of dollars as reparation to Israel due to the suffering Germany inflicted on the Jews. But the French continued to distrust Germany. To repair its relationship with France, Germany announced that the Ruhr region would be administered jointly by France, Germany, Belgium, Luxembourg, the United States, and the Netherlands. Appeased, France accepted the cooperation and started the economic unity of the western European nations. The 1950s also brought Germany other benefits, such as permission to rearm itself and join the North Atlantic Treaty Organization (NATO). But the culmination of the West Germany government's efforts to elevate the country's diplomatic status came in 1952 with the Bonn-Paris conventions. On May 5, 1955, the three western Allies agreed to grant the Federal Republic of Germany full sovereignty. Although the occupation of Germany was officially over, the Allies retained the right to administer western parts of Berlin and oversee the possible reunification of Germany in the future.

The acceptance of the Federal Republic of Germany into NATO resulted in a Soviet response. The Warsaw Treaty Organization was formed, better known as the Warsaw Pact. Founded on May 14, 1955, the pact gathered Communist states Albania, Bulgaria, Czechoslovakia, Hungary, Poland, Romania, East Germany, and Russia into a military alliance. The hopes of a unified Germany died with the Warsaw Pact, but the Adenauer government didn't give up. In September of 1955, West Germany issued the Hallstein Doctrine, which was used to prevent the international recognition of the GDR. The doctrine warned that the Federal Republic of Germany would stop all diplomatic efforts with nations that recognize the sovereignty of East Germany. Ulbricht responded with his own doctrine, which called for the members of the Warsaw Pact to refuse recognition of West Germany until Adenauer recognized the GDR.

The Berlin Crisis and the Unification of Germany

The Berlin Wall
Noir, CC BY-SA 3.0 <http://creativecommons.org/licenses/by-sa/3.0/>, via Wikimedia Commons https://commons.wikimedia.org/wiki/File:Berlinermauer.jpg

The divide between West and East Germany culminated in November 1958 when the new Soviet premier, Nikita Khrushchev, demanded that western Allies leave Berlin. He claimed Berlin wanted to become a free city, and he threatened that if the Allies didn't leave voluntarily, the Soviets would take the city in the name of the GDR. When NATO refused the Soviets' demands in December of the same year, the Berlin Crisis began. Unable to fulfill his threats, Khrushchev offered an alternative. He proposed a permanent division of German territories, with Berlin as a demilitarized zone. But NATO refused this proposal too, aware that the Soviet Union had nothing but empty threats. In the meantime, life in East Germany became unbearable due to the Communist regime, growing poverty, and lack of prosperity. The Germans started defecting from East Germany to West Germany in the hopes of a better life. By 1961, the number of defectors had risen above two million. To stop its people from escaping, the GDR began construction of the famous Berlin Wall— a barrier that separated the eastern part of the city from the western part for almost three decades. Although it no longer exists, the Berlin Wall remains a symbol of the oppressive nature of Communism. The wall didn't just divide the city: it also divided people. Families were torn apart as communication between the two parts of Berlin came to a halt. The GDR installed border police to guard the wall, and several hundreds of young people were killed trying to climb the wall and escape the regime, the ideology, and the political oppression.

But the wall was just a beginning. The GDR fortified the outskirts of the entirety of Berlin, including its western zone. The mayor of West Berlin, Willy Brandt, feared the city would be cut off from the rest of the world, and he called on the United States to help. For twenty-two months, Soviet and US soldiers stationed themselves on each side of the barrier, and the war was about to start. On June 23, 1963, US President John F. Kennedy came to Berlin and delivered his famous speech, "*Itch bin ein Berliner*" ("I am a Berliner"), promising support for West Berlin. This was enough to convince the Soviets that the United states was very serious in its intention to safeguard the western area of the city, and they gave up on their intention to send tanks over the border. Nevertheless, the unification of Germany was still very far away.

Although West Germany continued to prosper economically, the country reached its first crisis point. In 1968, radical student protests erupted as a response to campus unrest in the United States and France. The protests were organized against the United States' military efforts in Vietnam between 1965 and 1968. But the Vietnam War wasn't the only reason for discontent in West Germany. The young people started realizing that oppression continued in their home country through the restriction of the freedoms of the press and speech. The *Spiegel* Affair occurred earlier in 1963 when this German magazine dared to criticize the government. Adenauer ordered the police to raid the magazine's headquarters, and its publisher, Rudolf Augstein, was charged with treason for daring to publicly comment on Adenauer's security policies. The West German government was heavily criticized, and Adenauer was forced into retirement. The next chancellor elected was former Nazi official Kurt Georg Kiesinger. The youth of West Germany were astounded that their government would allow a former Nazi to enter politics again. The leftist student organizations started violent protests throughout the country, blaming defective German society for the government's hypocrisy. The students accused their government of having an authoritarian nature and of being unable to atone for its Nazi past. They also blamed it for having too much faith in the capitalist economic system, which was, in their eyes, a moral ruin. Students demanded democratic changes on all levels of the government. To quell the increasingly violent uprising, West Germany's government passed the German Emergency Acts by which the executive branch was empowered to operate without the approval of the legislative body. The Acts also restricted some of the constitutional rights of the citizens and approved the use of military force to restore order in the country. The Emergency Acts were very much like Article 48, which Hitler had used to elevate himself as the Nazi dictator.

The leftists started influencing the politics of West Germany during the late 1960s. Their growing popularity helped end the CDU's monopoly on political power in the government. In the Bundestag elections of 1969, the SDP ran a close second to the CDU, but once the SDP entered a coalition with the Free Democratic Party (FDP), Socialist leader Willy Brandt (former mayor of West Berlin) became the new chancellor. He abandoned the politics of the Hallstein Doctrine and implemented the policy of Ostpolitik, seeking to work closely with the GDR and the allies of the Warsaw Pact to establish fruitful diplomatic relations.

Ostpolitik was a complete turnaround and a move away from the conservative politics of the Adenauer government. In the past, West

Germany wouldn't even consider recognizing the GDR as a legitimate state, but now, in the early 1970s, Brandt sat at the same table with the GDR's minister-president. Although nothing much was achieved during the first meeting, the path to the establishment of formal relations was paved. Brandt also negotiated a treaty with the Soviets, the Moscow Treaty, by which the signing partners were to avoid military conflict and respect the existing European borders. The diplomatic efforts of the West German chancellor succeeded when the Soviets agreed to guarantee free access from West Germany to West Berlin. Willy Brandt received a Nobel Peace Prize in 1971 due to his work in establishing diplomatic relations between the two Germanies. But this was not the end of his success. In 1972, the Federal Republic of Germany and its eastern counterpart, the German Democratic Republic, signed the Basic Treaty by which they recognized each other's sovereignty. They also guaranteed to maintain peace between themselves, beginning an era of successful dialogs, diplomatic visits, trading relations, and cultural exchange.

But Brandt's political opposition, the members of the CDU and FDP, accused his Ostpolitik of being traitorous. The chancellor himself was accused of collaborating with the GDR, and on April 24, 1972, the government authorized a vote of no confidence to remove Brandt from the office. But the opposition failed by only two votes. The chancellor's reputation was further eroded by the tragedy which occurred during the Olympic Games of 1972. A Palestinian terrorist organization known as the Black September raided the Olympic Village in Munich where the athletes were housed, taking Israeli contestants and their coaches as hostages. They demanded the release of more than 200 Palestinian militants who were imprisoned in Israel and also demanded incarcerated leaders of the Red Army Faction be released from West Germany's prison. Two months later, in the new elections, Brandt and his party managed to secure a victory. Serving as a chancellor once more, he continued his diplomatic mission to connect West and East, and he extended a peaceful hand towards the nations of the Warsaw Pact, creating diplomatic relations with Hungary, Czechoslovakia, and Bulgaria. In 1973, Both Germanies joined the United Nations. But another crisis hit West Germany when oil prices skyrocketed due to the unrest in the Middle East. The "miracle economy" of the West showed exactly how fragile it was during a crisis, and more than one million West Germans lost their jobs by 1975. That number doubled by the 1980s. But Brandt was completely discredited in 1974 when one of his close associates turned out to be a spy, working for the secret police of the GDR. There was no recovery for the chancellor's reputation, and he had to resign. His replacement was another member of the SDP, Helmut Schmidt.

Even though Schmidt proved his capability in dealing with a terrorist attack in 1977 known as the German Autumn, his reputation suffered greatly due to the economic crisis in the mid-1980s. After the massacre during the Olympic Games, Schmidt organized a special anti-terrorism unit known as the GSG 9. He used them to save the hostages of the hijacked Lufthansa airplane in 1977 when another terrorist crisis occurred. Again, the Palestinian terrorists demanded the release of Red Army leaders, but the GSG 9 assault team stormed the plane on October 8, 1977, rescuing the hostages and killing or arresting the terrorists. But the economy of West Germany continued its downfall, and the working class was on the brink of an uprising due to unemployment when the CDU opposition called for a no-confidence vote. This time they succeeded, and Schmidt had to abandon his position as chancellor of West Germany. His replacement was CDU member Helmut Kohl.

Kohl's politics were completely different from his SDP predecessors. Instead of continuing the diplomatic relations with the East, he turned to Germany's western allies. First, he allowed NATO's nuclear warheads to be stored on German soil, and then he worked on tightening relations with France. In 1984, he met with the French president in a ceremony that was staged as a reconciliation for the bloodshed between the two nations during both World Wars. This ceremony, held in Verdun, is considered the foundation of future European integration. But during his second mandate, which started in 1987, Kohl reversed his policy again and started building relations with the Eastern Bloc. He invited the East German leader, Erich Honecker, to visit West Germany—the first eastern official to do so. All of Eastern Europe's Communist regime was under enormous pressure as its citizens pressed for democratic reforms. Individuals appeared who were able to expose the corruption of the Communists, pressuring the government to negotiate. One such incident occurred in Gdansk, Poland, where a non-governmental trade union rose from the shipyards. The idea that organizations were not controlled by the government quickly spread to the Eastern Bloc and, in 1984, reached the GDR. By that time, East Germany was facing a serious economic crisis.

In the GDR, the Communist regime failed to provide for its people. The idea of production quotas proved to be impossible to carry the economy of the whole country, and the first to suffer this failure was the working class. The living conditions in East Germany were falling rapidly. Supply shortages imposed hunger on people, and some of the survivors still testify to the inability to buy basic ingredients to sustain a family. But it wasn't only the economics of the GDR that bothered its people. The government oppressed its people, and it did so through espionage and strict control. The government had a file on everyone, and everyone's phones were tapped—even the public phones on the streets. Practicing religion was frowned upon, and those who went to church were forbidden from receiving higher education, as they were considered politically inappropriate—even children. People's mail was read by the government, and it would often not be sent because it was considered dangerous information leakage. Many East Germans had brothers, sisters, mothers, and fathers in the West, and they couldn't even communicate with them. All of this was too much for people, and during the 1980s, many of them sought asylum in foreign countries. On January 15, 1986, angry protests occurred in the GDR, with the people demanded changes. But Erich Honecker pronounced the protests illegal, and many of its participants were arrested and sentenced to prison. When, in 1985, Mikhail Gorbachev became the general secretary of the Communist Party of the Soviet Union and started reforms, the whole Eastern Bloc began to falter.

In 1988, Gorbachev announced that the Soviet Union was abandoning the Brezhnev Doctrine implemented twenty years earlier, by which it had guaranteed military intervention to preserve Communism in the members of the Warsaw Pact. This meant that each country was now free to pursue the political direction it wanted. The people in the Eastern Bloc organized a demonstration demanding change. One after another, the Communist regimes of Eastern Europe fell. In August of 1989, Hungary opened its borders with Austria, and the Germans from the Eastern Bloc took the opportunity to run to the West. But the government of East Germany responded by suppressing the demonstrations, drawing worldwide criticism. Feeling the support of the world, the people continued their efforts to fight for freedom. The situation was out of the government's control, and finally, on October 18th, the German people ousted Honecker. On November 4th, Berlin was a city of massive demonstrations that succeeded in persuading the government to back down another step: it officially proclaimed freedom of movement for East Germans. Over the next few days, an incredible crowd gathered along the Berlin Wall, and the border police had no other choice but to open the crossing.

Once on the other side of the wall, Eastern Germans were welcomed by a cheering crowd of westerners and their long-lost friends and family members. Scenes of the reunions behind the wall were quickly broadcast all over the world by various news agencies, and the whole world celebrated. The wall, once a symbol of separation and oppression, now meant nothing. The Communist government of the GDR fell, and the free elections were about to be held for the first time. But Helmut Kohl saw the opportunity to unite the two Germanies. At the end of November, he reached out to Eastern Germans with a ten-point plan offering them generous economic aid as well as cultural and social exchange. His plan was the foundation on which the future German Federation would be built. The next year new democratic parties arose in East Germany, including New Forum, Democratic Awakening, and Democracy Now. These parties were essential to securing fair democratic elections in the future, and East Germany was finally moving towards complete democracy.

In 1990, Kohl traveled to the Soviet Union to meet Gorbachev and discuss the reunification of Germany. Once the German chancellor promised that united Germany would not be any threat to the Soviet Union, the Russian premier announced that he would not stand in the way of reunification. But Kohl also had to secure the acceptance of the reunification from the western powers. Europe was still insecure about Germany's past and fears of another major crisis, such as world war, had to be dealt with. The German chancellor proved capable of securing the approval of the western Allies (the United States, Britain, and France), and on May 18, 1990, the two Germanies signed an agreement to join their economies. Not long after, on August 31, 1990, the Unification Treaty was signed, and East and West Germany were officially united into a single nation. The new country fell under the federal constitution, and Berlin was chosen as its capital. It was decided that the new German nation would remain a member state of the UN, NATO, and the European Economic Community (EEC). The powers that administered Germany after World War II—Britain, the United States, France, and the Soviet Union—signed a Treaty of the Final Settlement on September 12, 1990, removing the remaining restrictions of Germany's sovereignty in place since World War II. The new Germany was born, and it would again take its rightful place on the stage of the world's politics.

The only thing remaining to remind the people of the deep divide caused by the consequences of World War II was the Berlin Wall. Although it was filled with holes made by a bulldozer as the people opened the way to their western cousins, parts of it remained standing until 1991. A symbol of division, oppression, and bitter German history, the Berlin Wall was a place where many famous people of the time gathered to deliver hope for a better future— from various politicians to American presidents and famous artists. Singers such as David Bowie and Bruce Springsteen had held concerts near the wall so they could be heard by the people of both sides (1987 and 1988, respectively). They sang songs of freedom and unity, inspiring people to fight for their rights. On New Year's Eve in 1989, David Hasselhoff held a concert suspended above the wall, celebrating the upcoming unity. Both West and East Berliners climbed the wall, celebrating the end of a dark era for Germany. The demolition of the wall started as soon as Germany was united and was completed almost a year later, in November 1991. Parts of it still stand as monuments, a warning to humanity not to repeat the mistakes of war and division. In some places where there is no more wall, a line is drawn to symbolize the oppressive past of one nation. Parts of the wall were even transported to various cities around the world to be displayed in museums, city squares, universities, government buildings, etc. Every continent in the world has at least one piece of the Berlin Wall. This way, everyone can witness it and learn from Germany's darkest days.

Contemporary Germany

In 2019, Germany celebrated thirty years since the fall of the Berlin Wall, but the differences between the western and eastern parts of the country are still visible. Many cultural differences divided the people. But with each passing year, and with the birth of new generations, the cultural gap is becoming almost invisible. Still, the economic gap is impossible not to see. Even today, wages are 20% lower in the east than in the west. No major modern company wants to open its headquarters in the eastern parts of Federal

Germany. When the unification started, in only several years most of East German's industrial sector was privatized. But it was a failed Communist dream and could not survive the economy of capitalism that ruled the rest of the country. Factories shut down, and millions of people lost their jobs, forced to move to the west to find new employment. The east was left abandoned, unable to progress and develop. German Federation continued to invest in its eastern states, and although in time the economy recovered, it still lags behind western Germany. Nevertheless, the German people managed to build a new Germany, one where it didn't matter if you were from the west or the east.

But building a new country didn't come without any controversies. The first one arose immediately after the reunification when the new capital had to be chosen. Westerners were reluctant to abandon their previous capital, Bonn. But finally, a year later, a vote was held, and the majority decided that the capital should be moved to Berlin, a city which was a historical legacy of both Germanies. Another crisis occurred with the integration of East Germany into the capitalist economy of the Federal Republic. The country had been bound by the same currency since the economic treaty signed before unification, but East Germany was unable to follow the example set by the industrial sector and production of its western brother. Enormous amounts of money had to be invested in modernizing industries, infrastructure, and communication systems of the eastern states, and at times it seemed as if the former GDR was a hole without a bottom that sucked money from the Federal Republic. Despite the huge investment in the former GDR, many easterners were resentful of western politicians taking positions within the government, education, and business. It seemed that all the best career positions were occupied by westerners who were educated in a completely different system. The people of former East Germany were unable to grasp capitalist ideals and suffered the loss of social security benefits guaranteed by the Communists. The unification of

Germany failed to live up to their expectations. But the government didn't want to give up. In 1992, it came up with the Solidarity Pact, which included tax hikes used to help with the rejuvenation of East Germany.

Instead of concentrating only on its internal problems, the Federal Republic of Germany proved capable of developing further international diplomacy. In fact, since the reunification, Germany was the leading force behind European integration. The plan was to work with its neighbors to construct strong economic and political ties. In November of 1993, Germany signed the Maastricht Treaty, forming the European Union (EU). In 1951, France and Germany had signed the Treaty of Paris, founding the European Coal and Steel Community. This grew into the European Economic Community (EEC) in 1957 when Belgium, the Netherlands, Luxembourg, and Italy joined France and West Germany. But in 1993, the European family grew even more, with Denmark, Ireland, Greece, Spain, the United Kingdom, and Portugal joining the economic and political partnership of the European Union (EU). The unification of Europe had expanded beyond simple economic deals, and member states now enjoy coordinated European diplomacy, justice, immigration policy, and defense.

As the differences between West and East Germany began to dissipate, the first German chancellor born in the GDR came to power: in 2005, Angela Merkel won the popular vote. Besides having been raised in the East, she also became Germany's first female chancellor. Angela studied physics and earned a doctorate in chemistry at the Academy of Sciences in Berlin, but while only a student in 1989, she became interested in the political transformation of Eastern Europe, which also swept her own country. After the fall of the Berlin Wall, she joined the Democratic Awakening party, and after the unification of the country, she joined the cabinet of Helmuth Kohl. But she became a more prominent public figure with her new appointment in 1994 as the minister of environment and nuclear safety. In 1998, when Kohl was ousted,

Merkel became secretary-general of the CDU. Under her direction, this political party was rejuvenated and, in 2000, became the head of the party. Nevertheless, when the elections in 2002 came, Merkel wasn't chosen as the opposition to chancellor Schröder, even though she was already very popular with the people. As a vocal critic of Schröder's politics, she did manage to place herself as the opposition candidate in 2005, winning to become the new chancellor of Germany. At the dawn of the 21st century, Merkel proved a capable leader of a nation that proudly emerged from its dark past. She worked on improving diplomatic relations with the United States and continued Germany's role in the EU, the UN, and NATO. In fact, she was proclaimed *de facto* leader of the European Union and the longest-serving head of a government within the EU. *Forbes* Magazine named her the most powerful woman in the world fourteen consecutive times and the second-most powerful person in the world, just behind Russia's President Vladimir Putin. With Angela Merkel, the politics of Germany became an integral part of the politics of the EU. She served as the president of the European Council and used this position to start reform within the European Union. The 2007 Lisbon Treaty serves as the constitution of the EU, strengthening its political and economic coherence. For her role in the Lisbon Treaty, Angela Merkel was given the Charlemagne Prize in 2008, which has been awarded by the German city of Aachen since 1950. The award is given to individuals who, through their performance, have brought about Europe's unity. Since then, Merkel has received numerous prizes all over the world. From the United States to India, she is recognized as a "leader of the free world." Remembering her life behind the Berlin Wall of post-war Germany, Merkel fights to destroy the walls, figurative and literal, which continue to divide people across the world. In her own country of Germany, Merkel was given the nickname "Mutti," a German word children lovingly use to call their mothers.

Conclusion

Germany succeeded in shaking off the weight of its turbulent past, and today, it is a federal parliamentary republic. Germany is a multicultural country, as it welcomes many migrants from the Mediterranean, Eastern Europe, and the rest of the world. In 2015, a new migration crisis hit the continent as millions of refugees poured in from the Near East. Germany proudly opened its doors, inviting many of them to find permanent new homes within its federal republic. Germany even changed its laws to make it easier for foreigners to gain citizenship. The new leaders of Germany see strength in diversity, even though that same diversity is not without its controversies.

Germany has placed itself among the leading nations of the world and is a confident and brave member of NATO, Group of Eight (G8), and the EU. It continues to grow economically and is at the top of the list of the richest nations in the world. But its main importance lies in its diplomatic efforts, as Germany has taken the key position in European affairs and built strong relationships with various countries across the world. The new Germany embraced liberal democracy after centuries of constant conflict and autocratic rule. Even though Germany went through years of oppression of racial minorities and the division of its nation, today it is one of the most liberal and democratic countries in Europe.

The German people reevaluated what it means to be German, and through a different kind of unity—one based on a shared set of civic values—it came to accept other ethnicities under its wing. To be German today means much more than to speak the Germanic language or have racially pure blond hair and blue eyes. Being German is about freedom, tearing down walls and cages that separate and enslave whole nations, and respecting the rights of all human beings. Through thousands of years-long history filled with tragedies, triumphs, bloodshed, and shame, the Germanic peoples have gathered experiences and have used them to create the modern-day state of Germany.

Here's another book by Captivating History that you might like

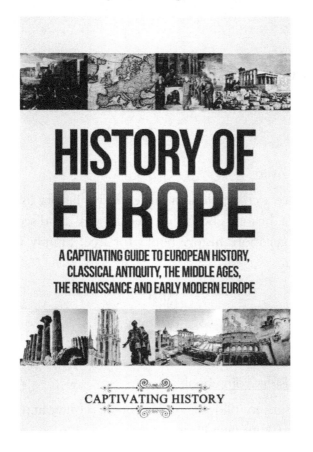

Free Bonus from Captivating History (Available for a Limited time)

Hi History Lovers!

Now you have a chance to join our exclusive history list so you can get your first history ebook for free as well as discounts and a potential to get more history books for free! Simply visit the link below to join.

Captivatinghistory.com/ebook

Also, make sure to follow us on Facebook, Twitter and Youtube by searching for Captivating History.

References

Acton, John Emerich Edward Dalberg Acton, Ward, A. W., Prothero, G. W., & Leathes, S. M. (1969). *The Cambridge modern history, volume 4, the Thirty Years War.* Cambridge: Cambridge University Press.

Blackbourn, D. (1998). *The long nineteenth century: A history of Germany, 1780-1918.* New York: Oxford University Press.

Boog, H., Krebs, G., & Vogel, D. (2015). *Germany and the Second World War.* Oxford: Oxford University Press.

Brecht, M. (1985). *Martin Luther.* Minneapolis: Fortress Press.

Carlyle, T. (1969). *History of Friedrich II of Prussia called Frederick the Great.* Chicago: Univ. of Chicago Press.

Collinson, P. (2004). *The Reformation: A history.* New York: Modern Library.

Cunliffe, B. W. (2003). *The Celts.* Oxford: Oxford University Press.

Curtis, B. (2013). *The Habsburgs: The history of a dynasty.* London: Bloomsbury Academic.

Fichtenau, H., & Munz, P. (2000). *The Carolingian empire.* Toronto: University of Toronto Press in association with the Mediaeval Academy of America.

Fisher, T. (2001). *The Napoleonic wars: The rise of the Emperor 1805-1807.* Oxford: Osprey.

Hart, D. (2014). *Calvinism A History.* Cumberland: Yale University Press.

Haverkamp, A. (1992). *Medieval Germany: 1056-1273.* Oxford: Oxford University Press.

Herwig, H. H. (2014). *The First World War: Germany and Austria-Hungary, 1914-1918.* Bloomsbury USA Academic.

Holborn, H. (1982). *A history of modern Germany.* Princeton, NJ: Princeton University Press.

Leyser, K. (1982). *Medieval Germany 900-1250.* London: Hambledon Press.

Regino, Adalbert, & MacLean, S. (2009). *History and politics in late Carolingian and Ottonian Europe: The chronicle of Regino of Prüm and Adalbert of Magdeburg.* Manchester: Manchester University Press.

Stearns, P. N. (1974). *1848: The revolutionary tide in Europe.* New York: Norton.

Unterreiner, K., & McGowran, M. H. (2011). *The Habsburgs: A portrait of a European dynasty.* Vienna: Pichler.

Warner, P. (2008). *World War One: A chronological narrative.* Barnsley: Pen & Sword Military.

Whaley, J. (2013). *Germany and the Holy Roman Empire.* Oxford: Oxford University Press.

Wilson, P. H. (2017). *The holy Roman empire: A thousand years of Europes history.* London: Penguin Books.

Wolfram, H. (1997). *The Roman Empire and its Germanic peoples.* Berkeley, CA: University of California Press.

Made in United States
North Haven, CT
27 April 2024

51850278R00104